THE SUNDAY TIMES

YOU CAN DO IT TOO

The 20 essential things every budding entrepreneur should know

Rachel Bridge

KOGAN PAGE

London and Philadelphia

Publisher's note
Every possible effort has been made to ensure that the information contained in this book is accurate at the time of going to press, and the publishers and author cannot accept responsibility for any errors or omissions, however caused. No responsibility for loss or damage occasioned to any person acting, or refraining from action, as a result of the material in this publication can be accepted by the editor, the publisher or the author.

First published in Great Britain and the United States in 2008 by Kogan Page Limited

120 Pentonville Road
London N1 9JN
United Kingdom
www.koganpage.com

525 South 4th Street, #241
Philadelphia PA 19147
USA

© Rachel Bridge, 2008

ISBN 978 0 7494 5153 0

The views expressed in this book are those of the author, and are not necessarily the same as those of Times Newspapers Ltd.

British Library Cataloguing-in-Publication Data

A CIP record for this book is available from the British Library.

Library of Congress Cataloging-in-Publication Data

Bridge, Rachel.
  You can do it too : the 20 essential things every budding entrepreneur should know / Rachel Bridge.
      p. cm.
    ISBN 978-0-7494-5153-0
1. Entrepreneurship. 2. New business enterprises. 3. Success in business. 4. Businesspeople. 5. Entrepreneurship–Case studies. 6. New business enterprises–Case studies. I. Title.
    HB615.B748 2008
    658.1'1--dc22
                                                2008017635

Typeset by Saxon Graphics Ltd, Derby
Printed and bound in India by Replika Press Pvt Ltd

For Harry

Contents

Acknowledgements   *x*

Introduction   **1**

1. **Find a niche**   **5**
    Profile: Giles Henschel, founder of Olives Et Al

2. **Choose a good name**   **13**
    Profile: Ross Lee, founder of The Barcode Warehouse

3. **Be clear what you are trying to achieve**   **21**
    Profile: Thea Green, founder of Nails Inc

4. **Get a mentor**   **29**
    Profile: Sanjay Bhandari, founder of Farmacia
    Urban Healing

5. **Do proper research**   **37**
    Profile: Adam Pritchard, founder of Pomegreat

6. **Find a business that can be scaled up**   **45**
    Profile: Oliver Brendon, founder of ATD Travel
    Services

7. **Protect your idea**   53
   Profile: Laura Tenison, founder of JoJo Maman Bebe

8. **Make sure the numbers add up**   61
   Profile: Loyd Hitchmough, founder of Cheshire Cookers

9. **Get your timing right**   69
   Profile: Jan Smith, founder of EOL IT Services

10. **Test your commitment**   77
    Profile: Annabel Karmel, founder of Annabel Karmel group

11. **Learn to love technology**   85
    Profile: Richard Downs, founder of Iglu.com

12. **Think twice before parting with equity**   93
    Profile: Justine Cather, founder of Burnt Sugar

13. **Don't assume your customers will find you**   101
    Profile: James Murray Wells, founder of Glasses Direct

14. **Think big**   109
    Profile: Hilary Devey, founder of Pall-Ex

15. **Make it easy for luck to strike**   117
    Profile: James Hibbert, founder of Dress2Kill

16. **Learn how to sell**   125
    Profile: Robyn Jones, founder of Charlton House

17. **Start networking**   133
    Profile: Neil Duttson, founder of Duttson Rocks

18. **Build a strong team around you**   141
    Profile: Sean Phelan, founder of Multimap

19. Learn from your mistakes   **149**
Profile: David Speakman, founder of Travel Counsellors

20. Accept that it will always take longer than you think   **157**
Profile: Edward Perry, founder of Cook

Appendix: Useful websites   *165*

Acknowledgements

It has been a real adventure writing this book and there are lots of people who have been a great source of help and inspiration to me along the way. Thank you to all the entrepreneurs and advisors included in this book for their time and generosity in sharing their experiences. Thank you to Jon Finch and everyone at Kogan Page for once again being brilliant in every way. Thank you to *The Sunday Times*, especially Editor John Witherow, Business Editor John Waples and Managing Editor Richard Caseby. Thank you also to Kathleen Herron for her encouragement.

I would also really like to thank all the entrepreneurs and small business owners I have met over the past few years at conferences and events around the country who have taken the time to share their thoughts and experiences with me. Finally I would like to thank my family and friends for their support and good advice. And a big hug to Harry, just for being there.

Rachel Bridge
London

Introduction

Starting up your own business is one of the most exciting, fulfilling and life-affirming things you can ever do. If you get it right, it will put you in control of your own destiny and give you a sense of achievement like nothing else can. It may also make you extremely rich.

Unfortunately starting up a business is also one of the most unpredictable things you can ever do and one that is statistically far more likely to end in failure than success. So how can you shift the odds in your favour? The answer is to learn from the people who have done it before you – as much as you can and as quickly as you can.

As Enterprise Editor of *The Sunday Times* I have spent the past few years talking to hundreds of extremely successful entrepreneurs about how they achieved their success. What they did right, what they did wrong, how they overcame problems and what they have learnt. Over that time I discovered that while each entrepreneur achieved success in their own unique way, their journeys shared several common traits. Traits that could be of enormous interest to a budding entrepreneur in search of guidance.

This book brings together the collective knowledge and wisdom of these successful entrepreneurs in an easily accessible way. From their combined insights and experiences I have drawn up a blueprint of the 20 essential elements you need to focus on when starting up a business. Every chapter takes one vital ingredient of becoming a successful entrepreneur. It looks at why it is important and how you can incorporate it into your own business venture. Each chapter ends with a profile of a successful entrepreneur illustrating how that essential element works in practice.

The result is effectively a masterclass for budding entrepreneurs. These people have made the mistakes, so you will know what to look out for and will have a better chance of avoiding similar errors yourself. They have found the shortcuts, so you can follow them instead of going all round the houses. The bottom line is that this book will save you years of wasted effort. This is your fast track priority boarding pass.

Of course dreaming about becoming an entrepreneur and then doing absolutely nothing about it is easy. So easy, in fact, that millions of us do it all the time. The hard part is taking the first step. In fact even working out what the first step should be can be pretty overwhelming in itself.

So regard this book as the first step. It is for anyone who has ever dreamed of starting up their own business but has no idea where to start or what is involved. It is for the person who is stuck in a dull nine to five job but dreams of being their own boss. It is for the person who has been made redundant and realises they still have the chance to do something special before it is too late. It is for the parent stuck at home looking after children who wants to start using their brain again. It is for the person who avidly watches *Dragons' Den* on television or reads the small business pages of a newspaper and thinks – that could be me.

Remember, all the entrepreneurs profiled in this book were once budding entrepreneurs too. They too started out with nothing but a good idea and a desire to succeed. Yet all of them have managed to create substantial businesses with a turnover of at least £3 million and in many cases much more. All of them used to be just like you and me. And just look at them now.

Jan Smith, the founder of EOL IT Services, which recycles old computers, is an almost textbook case of how to get your timing right when starting up a business. Giles Henschel, the founder of Olives Et Al, a business that sells nothing but olives, is proof that finding a niche can be an immensely sound strategy for a budding entrepreneur starting out. And Adam Pritchard, the founder of Pomegreat, the pomegranate juice drink, is a classic example of how proper research can pay off.

The entrepreneurs in this book also shed light on how not to do things. For example Laura Tenison, founder of JoJo Maman Bebe, the children's wear and maternity chain, found out the hard way how important it is to protect your business name. And Justine Cather who founded Burnt Sugar, which makes and sells fudge and old fashioned sweets, belatedly discovered that you should always think twice about parting with equity in the early stages of your business.

As well as the 20 entrepreneurs themselves a number of professional advisers, who between them have many years of experience of helping start-up businesses, share their views and advice. These include Doug Richard, a former judge on *Dragons' Den* and now the founder of Library House, a research company focusing on private businesses, and Kim Fletcher, an adviser from Business Link, the government-backed advice centre for small businesses.

As a budding entrepreneur you are about to enter a world you know very little about. That means you start with an instant disadvantage. This book will go a long way towards redressing that imbalance by giving you the tools and the knowledge you need to stride forth with confidence. And prove that truly you can do it too.

1

Find a niche

One of the most daunting aspects of starting up a business from scratch is the thought that you will be competing against much larger businesses that have been around for a lot longer and are far more established than you in the marketplace. But there is a brilliantly simple solution to this – do not compete against them. Instead find a small segment of the market that is either too small or too specialised for the big boys to bother with – and then waste no time in making it your own.

When it comes to business there are very few advantages of being small when everyone else around you is big. But one of those advantages is the ability to create a niche market for your product or service that the big players cannot enter, either because it is just not worth their while in terms of potential return or because they simply do not know how.

Take Bathstore.com, which sells nothing but bathroom accessories. Or Penhaligon's perfume shop. Or the Left Handed shop, which sells accessories for left-handed people. Or even the Ooze Risotto restaurant in London's West End, which sells 13 types of risotto. All have created successful businesses by focusing on a single product, and then making sure they know absolutely everything there is to know about that product. So that if a customer just has to have an all-day breakfast risotto then they will know exactly where to go.

Daniel Ronen, director of DoS UK business consultancy, says: 'The biggest mistake small-business owners make is to find themselves up against difficult competition because they are fighting against the big boys. The secret is not to go head to head with them. Instead of trying to compete against large organisations that have the advantage of economies of scale, try to change the game slightly. Offer what you are doing in a way that the large organisations cannot compete with or wouldn't want to compete with. You may want to provide different services or options, or change the way you deliver what you are doing.'

He adds: 'Being a small company means that you can get into markets that are not viable for large businesses. Big companies sometimes find that it is just not worth investing in a market because the returns would be too low to justify the effort. But as a small business you generally have a lower cost structure. So where markets are not big enough to support a number of large companies, smaller suppliers of niche products or services can make very good profits. The secret is to make sure that you play the game on your terms rather than theirs.'

The big advantage of finding a niche, of course, is that by offering a specialised service you are not only reaching the parts that the big players cannot reach – you are also able to get closer to your customers. That means you can focus your product or service in a way that really suits the customer and fits their needs. And so the more niche you are able to be, the better you are able to satisfy their demand.

And that heady combination of specialist knowledge and customer knowledge means you are likely to be able to charge a premium for your product. A specialist chocolate shop is able to charge a lot more for its high quality chocolate than the local supermarket, or even upmarket department stores, because of the depth of knowledge it can offer – for example being able to source particularly difficult to find cocoa beans, and knowing everything there is to know about where they came from.

As consumers become more knowledgeable about, and interested in, the products and services they are buying, it looks likely that the trend towards creating increasingly niche markets will continue. As Ronen says: 'People don't want generic solutions any longer. They don't want to have to mould themselves to what is available, they want to buy something that fits them.'

There are however some limits to how niche your niche can be if your business is to prosper. There is probably not a great deal of demand for gold-plated dustbins no matter how much specialised knowledge about gold-plated dustbins the person who sells them has. It is possible to be too niche. When you focus and refine your product or service to such a point that the market is not big enough to sustain your business and there are not enough people out there to buy your product or service – that is when you know you have gone too far.

In the City of London, Fazila Collins and Georgina Lang have managed to find a niche that suits them down to the ground. They have now opened the sixth branch of their food shop, Fuzzy's Grub, which specialises in selling Sunday roast lunch with all the trimmings in a sandwich. Customers choose from roast lamb, beef or pork, and can then put roast potatoes, vegetables, Yorkshire pudding, stuffing and even gravy in their over-sized bread roll.

Collins says: 'Lunchtime trade is such a competitive market we knew we had to do something to.stand out. You have to be different because there is so much choice out there. And we both liked Sunday roasts.'

Collins, who with Lang named the shop after their nicknames, Fuzzy and Grub, says there were several big advantages to creating a niche market: 'Fuzzy's Grub is popular because it is so different. We have never done any marketing – it has all been word of mouth. We have become a destination place as well and, although our shops are off the main thoroughfares, people will seek us out.'

So how do you go about creating a profitable niche of your own? The first step is to look closely at existing markets and see if there is a specialised need that is not being met. The second is to decide whether there would actually be enough demand for your niche product to enable you to make money. The third is to learn so much about your niche that you become the automatic first port of call for customers seeking your specialist product or service. In other words, if you are going to do it, do it well, do it thoroughly and do it convincingly.

Kim Fletcher, business adviser at Business Link in Kent, says that the secret to creating a successful niche market is to be constantly alert to new developments. 'The most important thing is to know what your customers are thinking and what is influencing their thinking. You have got to keep on top of things otherwise you might find that your widget is last year's widget.'

Top tip

Aim to become a specialist in your field.

Profile: Giles Henschel, founder of Olives Et Al

Giles Henschel began his career in the army. He enjoyed it immensely but after 10 years he decided it was time to do something new. Unfortunately he soon discovered he had no experience of the commercial world outside the army and after much fruitless job hunting he started working for a charity in Covent Garden.

A year later, in 1992, he married his girlfriend Annie and the two of them decided to give up their jobs and take a year off to travel around the world. 'We decided to sell everything and buy a couple of motorbikes, then start in Gibraltar and follow the coast round the Mediterranean', he says.

Travelling through countries such as Greece, Turkey, Lebanon and Egypt, they encountered olives everywhere they went. 'The one thing you could always find was olives, but there were hundreds of different varieties and styles and recipes', says Henschel. They started asking questions of the people who picked the olives and began to collect recipes.

The two of them ended up in Cyprus and liked it so much they decided to stay and get jobs with a holiday company. But when a friend of Henschel's called from Britain to ask if he wanted to set up a training business with him, they decided to go home.

They got back to the UK a few months later and instantly regretted it. 'It was miserable', says Henschel. 'The weather was diabolical and it was horrible to be back. We were flat broke and we ended up living in a grotty bedsit in Southampton. We were thoroughly depressed.'

In an effort to cheer themselves up they decided to buy some olives, bread and wine to remind them of their trip. It was a futile exercise.

'We scoured the markets and delis of Southampton but we couldn't find anything that matched what we had been eating. The olives we bought were horrible and salty and bitter.'

Then they realised that the olives they had bought were little more than the raw ingredient. They decided to improve them by using the recipes they had gathered.

'We bought some tins of olives and had them festering away in a couple of manky old buckets in the corner of our bed-sit', says Henschel. 'When people came round they would try them and say they were fantastic and that we should sell them.'

The couple decided to give it a go and spent £500, the last of their savings, buying olives and glass jars. When they had water-cured and fermented them they took a stand at the Rural Living Show in Bath to see if anyone would buy them. They did.

Henschel says: 'We came back with a pocket full of cash and a very light car and said: "Why don't we do that again?".' Without consciously looking for one, they had found an untapped niche market with fantastic potential. So they started preparing olives at home during the week and taking stands at craft shows every weekend to sell them.

Henschel continued to spend three days a week in London training businesses in leadership and management while Annie prepared the olives. But after seven months he realised that selling olives was a lot more fun than training people and so he quit his job and he and Annie started selling olives full time.

The two of them continued to sell their olives solely at shows but as word spread they started supplying shops. After two years they moved into industrial premises in Dorset and in response to customer requests started selling their olives by mail order too.

Henschel says: 'We didn't have much idea about margin or profit so we made it up as we went along. Our answer to almost all the questions people asked was yes, we will give it a go.'

One question he did not say yes to though was when the supermarkets asked him if he would supply the olives to them. 'We said no because the more we were learning about the food industry, the less we were attracted by the idea of doing things in huge volume for little money. We decided very early that we would support the independent trade in the high street.'

That philosophy also extended to buying the olives. Initially Henschel bought raw olives from importers in London but as the business grew he started to buy direct from growers in Greece. 'I wanted to make sure that the money we spent stayed in the communities we were relying on. It is not about the pure margin that we make. Having those sorts of values has become increasingly important to us.'

Olives Et Al now supplies independent stores across the country, including Fortnum & Mason, Harrods and Heals. Turnover is expected to be £7.5 million in 2008.

Now aged 44 and with two children, Henschel admits he is driven by the fear of failure. 'I always imagine that someone is about to pull the rug from under my feet', he says. 'I constantly think that other people are doing it much better than we are. That is what drives me on. If you asked me whether my glass was half empty or half full I would probably always say it is half empty.'

But more than that, he is motivated by the desire to make a difference. 'I really want to change attitudes about how food is manufactured and how it is retailed, right across Britain and beyond. I want people talking about the fact that if we don't use our independent stores we are going to lose them. That is what drives me.'

2

Choose a good name

Thinking up a name for your business can be one of the most enjoyable aspects of setting up your own venture, particularly if you consider a list of ideas with friends over a bottle of wine late into the night. It can also be one of the most frustrating when you discover the next morning that all you have managed to come up with is a piece of paper covered in utter rubbish and crossings out.

But while you may be tempted to leave it until the last minute and then use the first thing that comes into your head, remember that the name you choose for your business can play a key role in enticing potential customers to take a closer look – or drive them away for ever. What is more, once chosen it will be difficult to change so it is important you get it right first time.

Neil Taylor, Senior Consultant at the brand consultancy Interbrand, which thought up Ocado, HobNobs, Prozac and Ford Mondeo, says the name you choose should reflect the objectives of your business. He says: 'The mistake most small businesses make when they are thinking of names is to be emotional about it and just focus on personal preference rather than business strategy. But you have to look objectively at what the name is trying to achieve. Your name should tell the story of what's different about you – what your business does or the way you do business. The name is the first thing people encounter – you have an opportunity to give a message and you should grasp it. And don't choose a name that is too limiting because what you do in the future might change.'

Taylor says the best way of coming up with a good name is to start by thinking up lots of possible ideas: 'Come up with as many names as you can. It's much easier to get to a great name by thinking of hundreds and weeding out the duds than it is to agonise over finding the perfect one. So get friends round, ask experts, think about what people in other industries have done. Explore every idea.'

It also makes sense to draw up a shortlist of possible names rather than singling out just one because there may turn out to be reasons why you cannot use your first option. Taylor says: 'There are lots of things out of your control that can stop you using a good name. Someone else may have beaten you to it, or it may mean something embarrassing in a country where you are hoping to do business. Try not to get too attached to one name because it is usually the one that will get knocked out.'

Graham Green, founder of the marketing communications agency Meerkat and now a marketing consultant, knows from experience how important it is not to get too keen on a single name. He originally wanted to call his company Tiger, but a quick search on the internet revealed that there were already hundreds of listings for companies called Tiger.

He says: 'Don't get attached to a name because there is a 99 per cent chance that it has already gone. We looked at dozens and dozens of names, but if you search on the internet you will find that a lot of good obvious names have gone. That is why company names such as Consignia and Arriva are all made-up names.'

He briefly toyed with the idea of calling his company Thor or Vulcan but ended up calling it Meerkat after an industry colleague suggested it. He says: 'We thought right, we'll have that. We were looking for a name that would suggest we were quick on our feet and that we were team players. And if you look at what a meerkat does, they are the best team players in the world and they punch above their weight. It works wonderfully well.'

Interbrand's Taylor says it also helps if the name says something about what the company does. 'Descriptive names take less time and money to support', he says. 'If you choose a name like Carphone Warehouse – when the company started out it literally was a warehouse full of carphones – then your name has done the communications job for you. If you call your company something like Ocado, you will have to explain to people what it does by spending money on advertising.'

Try to avoid names that will date though – while Carphone Warehouse's name was originally ideal for its market, since then mobile phones have evolved in ways that few could have imagined and the concept of a 'carphone' is now incomprehensible to a new generation of mobile phone users. If you think some of your business will come from the Yellow Pages or other listings choose a name beginning with A. As a general rule, avoid initials – it is difficult to create a warm feeling about them. Check the name does not mean anything undesirable in a foreign language. And avoid complicated names of the sort that need to be spelt out before people get them right.

Rohan Blacker and Pat Reeves set up their home food delivery company Deliverance in 1987 and now serve

15,000 customers a week, dispatching meals across London by motorbike within 45 minutes of an order coming in. They make all the food to order in their three custom-built kitchens in central and west London from a menu that ranges from Chinese and Indian to Italian, sushi and salads.

They decided to call their company Deliverance after a friend came up with the name. Previously they had toyed with the idea of naming it World Food Express, Oriental Express or Hurry Curry. The company now has sales of £6 million and employs 50 people.

Blacker says: 'We thought Deliverance was a cracker of a name. It implies salvation and delivery and doesn't necessarily imply food so if we want to expand the business in other directions we could still use the name. These days people use the word Deliverance as a verb, as a noun and even as an adverb. It has worked really well for us.'

Meerkat's Green says it is best not to be too clever when choosing a name, pointing out that one company that called itself Black Hole inevitably disappeared into one. He says: 'If you want to build a brand, you need a name that is evocative. There are so many firms out there and so much stuff going on that if you come up with a good name then you are at least getting on to potential customers' radar.'

Once you have drawn up a list of possible names, the first step is to put them into several search engines on the internet to see what other companies and products out there already share the same name. If one or more names still look hopeful, the next step is to call Companies House or visit its website (www.companieshouse.gov.uk) to find out if the name has already been registered. If any names are still in the running, the third step is to check whether the internet domain name is still available and then to secure as many of the co.uk, com, net and even eu website address endings as you can.

Top tip

Avoid terrible puns when naming your business. People will remember you – but for all the wrong reasons.

Profile: Ross Lee, founder of The Barcode Warehouse

As the youngest of nine children Ross Lee enjoyed a huge amount of freedom while growing up. 'I had six older brothers and they always stuck up for me and protected me', he says. 'The front door would open at seven o'clock in the morning and I would go out with them, and we would come back when we were ready to. We made our own fun.'

Lee was born in Macclesfield and brought up in Nottinghamshire, where his father was a mechanical foreman on the railway. He says the family had little money to spare but they enjoyed a happy life. 'We had no money, but we made things. We built our own bikes.'

After leaving school at 16, Lee started working in a coalmine, but he did not like it and after a couple of years he got a job working in power stations as a welder. Because he did shifts he was able to pursue projects of his own in his spare time. 'I bought land, renovated property and sold cars', he says. 'I knew I could always turn my hand to other things to make money, as well as do my regular job.'

Then, in 1986, while still working at the power station, he started up a small label-printing business for his daughter Joanne to run. 'My daughter had left school and didn't really know what she wanted to do', he says. 'My brother builds labelling machines, and over a drink one night he said: "Why don't you have a labelling machine, so your daughter can run a labelling business?".' His wife did the accounts and Lee acted as manager and salesman in his spare time.

Eight years later, in 1994, he was made redundant from his job at the power station at the age of 45. Too young to retire, he had to decide what to do next. The answer lay right in front of him. By this time the labelling business was making barcode labels for local busi-nesses and had a turnover of £100,000. Lee decided it had the potential to grow much bigger and support him as well as his wife and daughter.

He says: 'We had a business that I believed could be a serious business. It had the smell of success.' So he wrote a three-year busi-ness plan and borrowed £60,000 from the bank, using the family home as security. 'Failure was not an option', he says. 'We had to go for it.'

Lee decided to call the business The Barcode Warehouse because the name was memorable – and because no one would ever guess that there was a small family business behind it because the name implied a much bigger operation. He also created a logo for it. He says: 'I believed we needed to brand the business so that as soon as someone has dealt with us they never forget the name.'

Within six months he knew he had made the right decision. Demand for barcode labelling was growing and when Lee realised that companies were starting to buy their own barcode printers, he started selling printers and scanners as well.

From there it was a short step to providing hardware and software systems that track barcodes. The company now sells all kinds of barcode and IT-related equipment. 'We have reinvented the business year on year', he says.

A big turning point came when Lee was asked to tender for a barcode-labelling system for the forensic science service at the Home Office. He won the contract and it transformed the company's prospects. Lee says: 'Winning something like that we realised that we had come of age and so we could go for anything.' Just four years after they built their first factory they had already outgrown it and had to build another one.

As the company expanded it also became more of a family business. Lee first brought in his son-in-law, then his other daughter, and then his son and other son-in-law.

He says working with family members has not been a problem because they all have different skills to offer. It has also helped that the business has never experienced a setback. 'If you were a struggling business, you would probably be arguing about whose fault it was. We have never had that problem', he says.

The Barcode Warehouse (www.thebarcodewarehouse.co.uk) now supplies barcoding and tracking equipment to Royal Mail that is used to track every mailbag in the country. In addition, its systems run the Home Office DNA database and the NHS's electronic case-note-tracking system.

The company has also developed a vibrant e-commerce business thanks to Lee's son, also called Ross, who has turned what was a fledgling website into a £4 million division. As a result the Barcode Warehouse now employs 50 people and in 2008 the company is expected to have a turnover of £15 million.

Lee is particularly proud that Adam Crozier, Chief Executive of Royal Mail, came to open The Barcode Warehouse's new e-commerce centre in Newark, Nottinghamshire, in recognition of the role that the company has played in creating labelling and tracking systems for Royal Mail. He says: 'He came and said thanks for the last 10 years and that he would like to work with us in the future, and it blew me away.'

Now 59 and married for 40 years, Lee credits his achievements to his open outlook on life, something that he thinks stems from the way he was brought up. He says: 'I am an opportunist who surrounds himself with the right people.'

For Lee, success boils down to three things: 'First, the customer is king. Second, people buy from people, so you need to sell yourself. Third, deliver what you say you're going to deliver.'

3

Be clear what you are trying to achieve

When you are starting up a business for the first time it can be frighteningly easy to lose sight of what you are actually trying to do. You may think you have it all worked out in your head but the moment you start telling other people about your plans – whether friends, family or advisers – you can guarantee they will start offering all kinds of suggestions and advice that can completely throw you off track.

The problem is that while some of these suggestions may well be brilliant, others will be utter nonsense. If you have a well thought out game plan it will soon become obvious which are which. If you do not then pretty soon you will have no idea which way is up.

And while your friends and family may be relatively easy to ignore, it will be far harder to keep your head when customers start asking if you can add a new feature or function to the product or service you are offering them.

Geoffrey Galitzine and Chris Waldron started up their glass recycling company, Smash and Grab, in 2006. They supply pubs and restaurants with a glass-crushing machine, which they designed themselves. They collect the crushed glass from the pubs and restaurants on a regular basis and their system is so efficient that they now have more than 200 customers including Young's and Fuller's breweries. In a short space of time they have built up a sound business with a strong focus. But their resolve is continually tested by customers who constantly ask if they will collect their cardboard waste for recycling as well.

Although at first glance it may be tempting to expand their business in this way, using the customer base they already have, Galitzine knows it would be a bad idea. He says: 'People say to us you are taking our glass so why don't you take our cardboard at the same time? But there are two good reasons why not – first of all we think we now know a lot about glass collection and how to do it efficiently. We have a dedicated truck which is geared entirely to glass and I think that with the best will in the world we would start missing collections or being late if we collected cardboard too. Second our machine is unique, it is patented and there is nothing like it on the market. There are plenty of cardboard crushing machines out there which are perfectly good so really all we would be doing is adding another collection service.'

He says there is enormous danger in losing the focus of a business: 'I think that if we diffused our attention on what we do really well, then our general level of service would go down. I think the businesses who really know what they are doing and focus on that are the ones that are successful.'

Before you can start protecting the focus of your business from distractions, however, you need to know exactly what it is. So get a piece of paper and write down your answers to the following. Are you going to be a product manufacturing business and get someone else to sell and distribute it, like Innocent smoothies or Gu Puds? Or are you going to be a distribution business and sell other people's products, like Homebase or Boots? Or are you going to both produce and distribute your products, like Amazon or Starbucks?

Who are your customers going to be – are you going to sell direct to retail customers, or just to other businesses? Or both? How are you going to sell your product – are you going to open a chain of shops or offer your product or service entirely via the internet? Are you going to focus on a particular sector, like garden centres or gym wear, or are you going to spread your product or service across several sectors, such as a consultancy might do?

There are dozens more questions like this and you need to know the answer to every one of them. Only then will you really understand from the inside out what your business is all about.

One good way to nail down the focus of your business is to try and explain in one sentence what it is about. John Thompson, National Business Advisory Partner at Baker Tilly, an accountancy firm, says that on one occasion he asked 13 directors of an established firm to do this – and got 8 completely different answers. The chairman of the company was not impressed.

He says: 'If you are trying to build a business you have got to be able to articulate very simply and very clearly what it is that you do. You need to have a clarity of message and clarity of purpose so that everyone in the business understands what they are doing and how they are doing it.'

Of course when you start out in business you cannot hope to get everything right first time. You will inevitably have to do some tweaking and even have major rethinks along the way. But throughout all this you have to hold on to your core vision of the business, otherwise you will flounder.

You also need to think about your end goal. Are you planning to grow your business as quickly as possible so you can sell it in five years' time and retire at the age of 40? Or are you planning to build up a solid family business that will provide employment for several family members for many years, which you will then eventually pass on to your children?

Thinking about selling your business before you have even started it up may seem like madness. But knowing what you eventually intend to do with your business will make a big difference to how you set it up, how you fund it and how fast you grow it. It is called planning your exit strategy and venture capitalists do it all the time when they are considering making an investment. So should you.

Steve Hinton, Executive Chairman of QED Consulting, a business consultancy, says that being focused requires more than just saying you want to do it and then hoping for the best. 'Ask yourself why are you running this business, what is the point? It sounds incredibly obvious but people sometimes don't think it through. Getting a focus doesn't just happen.'

Top tip

Make your focus robust by writing everything down. Keeping it all in your head is no use to anyone.

Profile: Thea Green, founder of Nails Inc

When Thea Green needed to raise some money to fund her nail salon venture she could not have chosen a better time to do it. It was 1999 and the height of the dotcom era and investors were falling over themselves to give her money, despite her total lack of experience.

'We would ask everyone we knew if they knew anyone with money to invest – and then we would just cold-call them', she says. 'We got so obsessed that we didn't meet anyone without seeing what they could do to help us.'

Pitching the idea of a nail salon during the dotcom era did have drawbacks, however. 'During that mad internet time every single guy we met said he would back us if we could put our business on the internet', says Green. 'We had to point out that we couldn't actually do a manicure on the internet.'

In the end she and her business partner managed to raise £200,000 from several people who invested a few thousand pounds each. The two of them did not put in any money of their own because they did not have any.

Brought up in Wirral, near Liverpool, Green learnt about business from both parents. Her father was a company director of Littlewoods, the retail group, and her mother owned a snooker hall. 'My brother and I used to have to empty out the fruit machines and count all the money. I remember thinking that was the best job in the world', she says.

Green worked from an early age, getting jobs on Saturday and in the evenings while still at school. 'I did everything from working in an old people's home to working in hairdressers, restaurants and bars', she says. 'I was quite money-motivated.' In the end her parents had to bribe her not to work so she could study for her GCSEs.

After leaving school at 18, Green did a degree in public relations and journalism at the London College of Fashion. On Friday afternoons she would help sort out clothes for the fashion desk at the *Daily Mail* newspaper and then *Tatler* magazine.

On graduating, she was offered a job with *Tatler* as Fashion Co-ordinator and gradually worked her way up to Fashion Editor at the age of 24. As part of her job she spent a lot of time in the United States on photo shoots and while she was there she started to notice the popularity of nail bars. 'Everyone got their nails done as soon as they arrived. It was a semi-glamorous service that you could have done very cheaply for about 10 dollars.'

Green mentioned the idea to a friend, Marie-Therese, who worked in advertising and the pair decided that it would be worth exploring whether the idea would work in Britain. 'We would talk about it and wonder why nobody else was doing it', she says. 'But in the back of our minds we always thought that something would happen which would mean it wouldn't make sense, that there would be a reason why a big cosmetics company hadn't done it. It just seemed a bit too good to be true.'

When they failed to discover a reason they started writing a business plan. 'Through sheer naivety we were always going to open a chain of nail bars. It was never going to be just one', says Green.

They also started holding focus groups to canvass people's opinions, which were extremely positive. When a property-developer friend found a site for their first nail bar on South Molton Street in London, they realised there was nothing standing in their way. So Green gave up her job to concentrate on making it work.

'It actually became a business before we set it up', she says. 'We were doing so well telling everyone that we were going to do it, we had to do it. People started asking us when we were opening.'

Green decided that the unique selling point of her nail bar would be to provide a fast manicure – in 15 minutes rather than the usual 50 minutes – at a charge of £10. Nails Inc opened for business in November 1999, and after being mentioned in a news item on Sky TV on the first day, had customers queuing round the block. 'People were waiting two hours for a 15-minute manicure', she says. 'It was bizarre.'

Within a few months Green and her partner had opened four more stores, with each one selling branded Nails Inc products along with manicures. 'We both wanted to build a brand. We were brand-obsessed', she says.

Nails Inc raised more money from wealthy investors and now has 40 nail bars in Britain, most of them located within department stores. Two years after the business was launched Marie-Therese quit the venture, leaving Green with a large minority stake in the company. Turnover in 2008 is expected to be £13 million.

Now 31 and married with two children, Green says the secret of her success has been to be clear right from the start about what she was trying to achieve – and to keep the business focused on what it does best. 'At Nails Inc we have remained very brand pure. We haven't got involved in doing eyebrows or facials. A lot of our competitors do add-on beauty services and I think it is greed. We are just nails and everything to do with nails.'

Green is motivated by the sheer enjoyment of creating a business from nothing. 'I like building it and seeing just how far you can push it', she says. 'Seeing one nail bar turn into two nail bars and then into ten. And I love learning a bit about everything. The really amazing thing about setting up your own business is that you are involved in everything.'

She has this advice to give budding entrepreneurs: 'When you are setting up a business a lot of people will say to you, there is a reason why someone hasn't done that, or someone else is doing it. My advice is to ignore those comments because it doesn't actually matter. If it is a brilliant idea then five of you will survive doing it. And if there is a reason why someone else failed at it then you will find that out very quickly.'

4

Get a mentor

The best thing about being an entrepreneur is that there is no one to tell you what to do. The worst thing about being an entrepreneur is that there is no one to tell you what to do. No one to explain how things work, why doing this could be a bad idea, why doing that could alienate your customers for ever – and why doing the other means that you will almost certainly go bankrupt.

Which is why most successful entrepreneurs have had a mentor at some point while they were starting up their businesses. The best kind of mentor is someone who has been there before. Someone who has years of business experience, ideally gained through starting up a business of their own. Someone who has good industry contacts that they are happy for you to tap into too and who is there to act as a sounding board for ideas – an impartial fount of wisdom to guide and advise and occasionally cajole. But someone who will ultimately be happy to stand back and let you make your own decisions.

It can be a huge shock setting out along the road to starting up your own business, particularly if you are leaving the comfort of paid employment, no matter how dull and restricting it was. Having someone to show you the ropes can help make the transition from employee to entrepreneur a lot less daunting.

Even better, surveys show that entrepreneurs who have a mentor are more likely to be successful than those who have not. A report by Barclays bank suggests that those with a mentor have a 20 per cent greater chance of survival than those without.

So where can you find one of these fabulous creatures? If you already know of a business person from your industry whom you respect and admire, perhaps having heard them speak at a business networking event, then you could do worse than approach them and ask if they would be prepared to meet you on a regular basis to provide guidance.

If you do not know anyone who would fit the bill then one of the cheapest and most accessible schemes for those starting out is the government-backed Coaching and Mentoring Programme – formerly known as the Up and Running Scheme. This is administered by Business Link and provided by local enterprise agencies. Under the scheme, entrepreneurs with businesses that have been running for less than two years are matched with a mentor whom they meet one-to-one for half a day each month over 18 months.

Barry Franklin, an adviser with Business Link for London, says having a mentor in the early days can be invaluable as entrepreneurs cannot hope to know every aspect of setting up a business. He says: 'It is hugely important to have someone to bounce ideas off. There are just so many pitfalls and so many ways you can go wrong – so having a mentor can be a great help. Entrepreneurs tend to be brilliant at production, average at administration, woolly at marketing and hopeless at finance. It is really useful to have an experienced person who can guide you as the business develops.'

A key benefit of having a mentor is that they can provide impartial advice – unlike, say, a friend or family member who may be too close to what is going on. Franklin says: 'A mentor can offer advice on two levels. One is his or her personal knowledge and experience and the other is access to other sources of advice, guidance and assistance that the entrepreneur would not have known about. As the mentor is not tied into the business they can give unbiased advice that is based purely on a consideration for the person who is trying to start up a business.'

Alice Asquith launched her company, Asquith, in 2001, selling a range of yoga clothes for women over 30. She started off selling her designs through mail order and has launched her collection in Britain and the United States. For a three year period, from preparing to launch her business through to it being up and running, Asquith had a one-to-one session every few months with David Jones, the Fashion Business Adviser at the Portobello Business Centre in west London. The arrangement was made through Business Link's mentoring programme.

Asquith says: 'Having a mentor has been vital because I knew nothing about the fashion world and had to learn fast. I didn't have a clue how to buy fabric, where to find a manufacturer, how the fashion season is structured, or about branding and marketing. David really helped me, particularly with marketing and manufacturing and on developing the brand, which was crucial.'

She adds: 'He also emphasised the importance of collaborating with other small businesses and of cross-promotion, so I have now made links with yoga teachers. He was there to advise and support me in every area. For me to have this mentoring programme meant that I was no longer on my own.'

Another option for entrepreneurs starting their own business is the free mentoring scheme set up by the National Federation of Enterprise Agencies called the Business Volunteer Mentors scheme. Funded by the Phoenix Fund through the Small Business Service, the scheme matches businesses with local mentors, typically people who started up a business of their own. They agree to be available to offer guidance for up to 24 days a year, depending on the needs of the entrepreneur.

George Derbyshire, Chief Executive of the National Federation of Enterprise Agencies, says: 'Starting your own business can be a lonely affair, especially if you have always been the employee of a company. All of a sudden you haven't got a support network, you haven't got the facilities of a big organisation, and your chums are not there for a chat. You are on your own.'

With a mentor on board, however, the outlook looks very different. Derbyshire believes a mentor can play a key role in ensuring the survival of a business. He says that a mentoring arrangement should be tailored to the needs of the entrepreneur: 'Sometimes it is a fairly intensive process over a short period of time. Other times it becomes a low-key but continuous relationship, in which they have a chat once a month when there is an issue to deal with. Often people just need someone to talk to. It is very much an individual process driven by the needs of the client.'

If you like the idea of having an online mentor who you never actually meet then a good way of doing this would be to sign up to Horsesmouth (www.horsesmouth.co.uk), a free online service that has been set up so that people can act as mentors and share their experiences with those looking for help and advice. There is a section dedicated to starting and running a business and hundreds of experienced business people and successful entrepreneurs have signed up to act as mentors to budding entrepreneurs. You can choose either to ask one-off questions or have an ongoing online conversation with a mentor in much the same way as you might do face to face.

Top tip

The old saying 'a problem shared is a problem halved' works in business too.

Profile: Sanjay Bhandari, founder of Farmacia Urban Healing

Starting up a business was a nerve-wracking experience for Sanjay Bhandari. When he opened his first integrated health centre in London's Covent Garden, it took a month before any customers came in. He says: 'People were saying, "What is this place?".'

Born and brought up in Leicester after his parents emigrated to Britain from India in the 1950s, Bhandari was a shy child. He was bullied at school until he learnt how to stick up for himself.

He says: 'I was thrust into this really big boys' school where it was survival of the fittest. There were lots of fights. I was bullied enormously in the first year but after that I learnt how to defend myself. I learnt to survive on my wits.'

His father ran a handful of small shops and market stalls selling clothing and from the age of nine Bhandari and his younger sister Meenu were required to help out on the market stalls when they were not at school. It was not much fun. He says: 'I hated working there because we always had to work during holidays and Christmas. I got paid for it but I begrudged it because everyone else was on holiday while I was working.'

He took a degree in food technology and engineering at Reading University and embarked on a career in the UK retail industry. He then spent eight years working for cosmetics companies overseas, in Paris, Hong Kong and Barcelona. The long hours took their toll and while Bhandari was in Barcelona he collapsed from exhaustion. He says: 'I had burnt myself out. It came to a point where I couldn't work and was bedridden for two weeks.'

He recovered with the help of acupuncture, herbal medicine and homeopathy. That gave him an idea, and when, in 1997 at the age of 33, he was made redundant, he decided to set up a health store in London's Covent Garden where customers could find both conventional and alternative medicines.

'I decided I would like to create an integrated health centre that would offer advice, products and services and practitioners on site', Bhandari says. 'I thought that there might be more people like me who were suffering from stress and overwork but who didn't know where to go or what to ask for.'

He called his business Farmacia Urban Healing after seeing the word Farmacia on pharmacies in Barcelona. Using £75,000 redundancy money, he found a site on Drury Lane in Covent Garden that already had an NHS pharmacy licence. Then he spent the next eight months fitting it out with the help of a £100,000 bank loan. He opened for business in August 1998 offering a range of therapies such as nutritional counselling, osteopathy, beauty treatments and organic skin creams. It took rather longer, however, for customers to find the shop.

Bhandari says: 'The first few weeks were very tense and precarious because people didn't know what it was. It was in an unusually designed space and looked like an optical laboratory in a glass box.'

Fortunately the design magazine *Wallpaper** heard about them via the architects that Bhandari had used for the shop, and declared Farmacia Urban Healing to be the herbal emporium of the future. He says: '*Wallpaper** did a whole page feature on us and said this is what the future of health could be. That really catapulted us to international attention. People started to come from all over the world.'

The business took off and in 2001 Bhandari opened a concession in Selfridges' London store. It has become one of the most successful concessions within Selfridges.

Bhandari was less successful with his decision to open a second concession in Selfridges' Manchester store two years later, however. After 13 months he was forced to close the outlet, losing £150,000 and a lot of wasted time in the process.

He says now: 'From that experience I learnt that sometimes it makes sense to turn down opportunities in order to move forward. You have to really think through the implications of anything that you do.'

Through a partnership with a US retail investor, Farmacia received investment to develop its branded products and by 2005 had opened a concession at Harrods. It was also asked by British Airways to develop a men's skin-care range for their First Class cabin, which was well received.

One of the things that has helped him since starting up his business, says Bhandari, has been having a mentor to guide him – in his case a former colleague called George Rozsa. 'He is a very knowledgeable and experienced business executive and has always been someone I could talk to about business issues. He has kept track of me for the past nine years and we talk once a week on the phone. It has made a big difference. There are lots of issues that come up which you can't discuss with your employees so you need someone objective who is outside of the business who can help you see things in a different way.'

As the company prospered Bhandari was able to buy back the shares owned by private investors. He and his family now own 80 per cent of the business which now has nine stores and in 2008 is expected to have a turnover of £9 million.

Now 44, Bhandari thinks the secret of his success is to be 'hyper resilient'. He says: 'You will take lots of knocks in business. There will be days when things don't go right but you have to persevere – and you have to have faith.'

He has this advice for budding entrepreneurs: 'Research your market properly, understand what cash flow means and do a proper financial plan. Make three plans – an optimistic one, a realistic one and a pessimistic one, and be prepared to weather the storm if it all goes pear-shaped.'

5

Do proper research

If you are itching to launch your new business then the thought of spending months with your nose in a pile of market reports is an extremely unappealing idea. For a budding entrepreneur, however, proper research is one of the most powerful tools you have at your disposal. It can make the difference between a business that has real potential and one that is destined to go nowhere.

Unfortunately there are no short cuts. Research does not simply mean asking your friends and family whether they would buy one of your products. Friends and family are a perfectly valid starting point, but proper research means analysing in depth your potential market, your competitors, trends within the industry and forecasts of its growth and likely direction.

The good news is that there exists an enormous amount of secondary research that has been done already which is out there just waiting for you to tap into. The even better news is that you can find out an enormous amount for free. The first place to go is your local library. If you are able to get to London, the newly opened Business and Intellectual Property Centre (BIPC) at the British Library (www.bl.uk/bipc) has a lot of resources available, most of it free, for people looking to set up their own business. If you do not know what you are looking for or where to start, the library staff can point you in the right direction. You can also book a free 30 minute advice session with a member of staff to go through in detail what you need and how to get the most out of it.

The information available includes 7,000 printed market-research reports, including Mintel and Frost & Sullivan. These cover every kind of market you can think of and give details of the major players, the size of their market shares, the sector's potential for growth and so on. The BIPC also provides free access to other resources that would normally be available only for an expensive subscription. These include Euromonitor, which has access to 4,500 country and industry lifestyle reports, and Key Note which has more than 2,000 reports covering 30 industry sectors.

In addition there are brokers' reports, which provide an in-depth assessment of markets, trade journals and business media. The Centre also runs weekly workshops that are either free or heavily subsidised. Topics include 'Researching a company' and 'A beginner's guide to intellectual property'.

Ben Sanderson, a spokesman for the British Library, says: 'Primary research can be very expensive and time-consuming, so if you consult some secondary research initially, you can develop a good understanding of the market and your customers and competitors. It is putting you in the best position before you spend any money.'

If you are unable to get to London, other libraries with good business resource centres include Norfolk and Norwich Millennium Library, Birmingham Central Library, Manchester Central Library, Scotbis at the

National Library of Scotland in Edinburgh, Leeds Central Library and Belfast Central Library. In Wales, Business Eye (www.businesseye.org.uk) has details of several business resource centres there.

You can also do a lot of free market research online, from finding out about seasonal trends and demographics in your market, to researching your rivals. Google Trends (www.google.co.uk/trends) can tell you at what time of year there is the biggest demand for your product. If you are thinking of starting a business selling lawnmowers, for example, it will show that each year there are three distinct spikes of demand, in April, May and August.

Microsoft is testing a new product that can give you a free breakdown by age and gender of who is searching for a particular product. Go to http://adlab.microsoft.com and click on the 'Intelligence' link. It will tell you, for example, that 78 per cent of people searching for 'garden shrubs' are female, a statistic that could be helpful in creating your business plan.

If you go to http://inventory.overture.com it will tell you how many times a month people have searched for a particular word on Yahoo, the search engine. There is no home page, just the tool, but it is a great rough-and-ready guide to how many people were searching for your product over a particular period. In a one month period, for example, 58,444 people searched for lawnmowers but only 973 searched for garden shrubs.

Researching your competitors online is also easy. Simply use a search engine to look for firms already doing what you want to do. Remember to search as if you were a customer. For example, search for 'drain unblocking' rather than 'high-pressure jetting' because customers tend to use descriptive terms rather than industry jargon.

If you are entering an established market, there are likely to be plenty of existing businesses with websites to trawl for information. You can find out how they describe what they do, how they package their services and the prices they charge.

Your research should not stop once you have launched your product or service. Fiona Davies, Membership Services Manager for Women in Rural Enterprise (WIRE), a networking group with 2,500 members, says: 'The best people to ask about your product are the people who have already bought from you because they are 50 per cent more likely to buy from you again. So keep asking them questions – if it is underwear, for example, ask them what they think about a nude colour for summer, or do they like plastic straps? Not only is that engaging them, it is also telling you what they want. The minute you decide that you know what your customers want and ignore what they are telling you, you are lost.'

She also advises becoming a customer of your competitors so you can keep an eye on what they are doing: 'The first thing WIRE ever did was sign up for another network.'

Judith Hunt and Steve Connelly launched their online trade exchange for businesses, Bizunlimited (www.bizunlimited.co.uk), in February after researching their idea for three years. Their research included using the free facilities at City Business Library (a public reference library in the City of London) to look at competitors' annual reports, finding out about other barter systems around the world and creating mailing lists of potential customers.

As part of their research, Hunt and Connelly took a stand at an exhibition and asked everyone who passed to fill in a questionnaire about the service they were planning to launch, offering them the chance to win an iPod as an incentive to complete it. Then they e-mailed everyone who had visited the show to get their views too.

Hunt says the negative feedback was just as useful as the positive responses: 'Some people were cynical about our service and so we were able to log a whole bank of objections to what we are doing. Then we wrote a list of 40 points of resistance and used them for our telephone scripts, in news releases and on our website.'

Hunt also quizzed the firms that joined Bizunlimited about how the service compared with that of its competitors.

Another useful place to start your research is Business Link (www.businesslink.gov.uk), the government-supported advice organisation for small firms. Its information service can tell you what research is available and how to get it. And if you decide you need to commission market research specifically relevant to your needs, Business Link advisers can help you draw up a brief and find a market researcher to do the work.

Top tip

Before you begin, write down a list of questions you hope your research will answer. It will help you stay focused.

Profile: Adam Pritchard, founder of Pomegreat

The first 24 years of Adam Pritchard's life were spent doing very little. Born and brought up in Bristol, he spent most of his time at school playing sport and when he left at 16 he lasted just eight weeks at college. For the next eight years he travelled the world,

returning home to the UK every few months to earn a bit of money doing casual jobs as a waiter. He says: 'I didn't really have a great many thoughts at that time other than having a laugh.'

When Pritchard eventually returned to the UK at the age of 24 he decided he wanted to become a stockbroker, so he took the Financial Services Authority exams and got a job with a stockbroking firm in London. Within weeks he realised he hated it.

He says: 'I wanted to be a stockbroker because I thought I could earn a lot of money and it would be really exciting doing all that trading. But in reality I was cold-calling customers and clients to try and pick up business.'

He was fired from the job. Undaunted, he decided to start up a car brokering business that would find cars for people. Unfortunately he did not know anything about cars and within three months he had gone bust, having lost £50,000 borrowed from friends or put on credit cards.

With no money and no job, Pritchard reluctantly returned to his original plan of becoming a stockbroker. But while he was retaking his out-of-date FSA exams, an old friend rang from Pakistan to say he had tasted a fantastic fruit juice made from pomegranates at a street stall and Pritchard should come and take a look. So Pritchard immediately caught a plane out there to try it for himself. He says: 'I know it sounds a bit strange that someone would just jump on a plane to go and see a fruit juice but to be honest I was pretty desperate because I didn't want to go back to the City.'

Pritchard tried the pomegranate juice and, although he personally did not think it was particularly amazing, realised that it could have big potential in the UK. On his return home he went to the British Library to do some in-depth research into pomegranate juice. 'I started to understand what the health benefits of pomegranates were and I thought it was fascinating,' he says. 'It was something that no one else was doing and yet it was so obvious.'

He initially started his venture with two friends but when they dropped out he continued on alone, making several trips to India to meet major fruit juice concentrate producers there. On his fourth trip he set up a trial to make pomegranate juice. It was an important moment. He says: 'I had already spent a year going to and from India and I was skint.'

The trial was a disaster. 'This pink gloopy mixture poured out of this machine onto the floor because they didn't know how to process it properly', he says. 'At that point I thought it was all over.'

Pritchard returned to the UK and in one last throw of the dice went back to the British Library, where he discovered that the only other country in the world that produced pomegranates in any volume was Iran. Unfortunately it was 2002 and Iran was just about to go to war with Iraq. But Pritchard was not about to let that stand in the way.

He says: 'It was not ideal, but I had come so far with it that to not get on a plane to Tehran would have been stupid.' He managed to get a visa and met the managing director of a factory there.

He says: 'He gave me this juice, I tasted it and it was great. It was exactly what I was looking for. It was like finding the Holy Grail.'

Pritchard came back to the UK and wrote a business plan, and then he managed to raise £150,000 investment from friends to get his business off the ground. He decided to import pomegranate juice concentrate from manufacturers overseas and blend it and package it here.

Then in 2003 he started selling his Pomegreat juice in Waitrose. But Pritchard had not got his figures right and after six months the business was on the verge of collapse.

He says: 'Everyone was patting me on the back saying hadn't I done well. But I realised we could go bankrupt because the cost of delivering the juice was almost the same as the price Waitrose was selling it for.'

In an effort to avert disaster Pritchard completely restructured the business, changing everything from his suppliers to the sales team. At the last minute the company was saved when Sainsbury's agreed to stock the juice, a deal which enabled Pritchard to raise another £140,000 investment from friends.

But there were more setbacks to follow. Pritchard put the wrong barcode on the cartons being sold in Sainsbury's, which meant they could not scan through the till for the first two weeks. He says: 'I got a phone call from the Sainsbury's buyer who said: "Adam, you have committed the cardinal sin in retailing." I thought, this really can't get any worse.'

By 2004, however, the business was starting to get on track. When a newspaper article extolling the virtues of pomegranate juice was published, sales of Pomegreat rose 600 per cent overnight. Tesco also began stocking the juice. As a result turnover in 2008 is expected to be £15 million.

Unusually, Pritchard, 33, runs the business as a virtual company, employing only himself and outsourcing all the other functions. Even the role of sales director is taken by an outside agency.

In sharp contrast to his earlier aimless years, Pritchard, who owns 27 per cent of the company, has now become driven by the challenge of succeeding. He says: 'I am very ambitious and very competitive. I won't take no for an answer.'

6

Find a business that can be scaled up

No matter how enthusiastic you are about starting your own business and no matter how much energy you are willing to commit to it, there is always one brick wall you are going to find yourself coming up against time and time again – the fact that you are only human. With the best will in the world you cannot be in two or more places at once, you cannot travel through time and you cannot work indefinitely without stopping at least once in a while for sleep, food and the occasional bath.

Which is why your business must have scalability. At its simplest scalability means that you do not actually have to be there to do the thing that makes the money. If your business is going to rely solely on your personal skills and expertise to create the product or service – for example, if you are a jewellery maker or a chef – then the business will not be scalable because its expansion will be limited by how much work you personally can do. That means you will only ever have a tiny business that has no scope to grow.

If, on the other hand, your business provides a product or service that other people can be trained to provide, for example an oven-cleaning service or a bespoke cake-making business, and there is potentially no limit to how many people you can recruit to do this – then you have a scalable business. Scalability means that your business can be expanded, potentially without limit. And that spells the difference between creating a business that will provide you with a modest living and one that could be sold for millions. That is a very big difference.

Daniel Ronen, director of DoS UK business consultancy, says: 'If a business isn't scalable then, quite frankly, only rarely should you go into it, because what you will be doing is creating a job for yourself rather than building a business that can be sold.'

He adds: 'If you are not able to scale up the business you will never be a true entrepreneur because you will always be caught in a cycle of "The more successful the business is, the busier I become, the more stressed I am, the less able I am to give my best". And if you are not giving your best the business will never truly grow. You get caught up in this dreadful loop and you will never be able to make the business fly.'

One entrepreneur hoping to make scalability work for him is Robin Barrasford, an overseas property agent who has just opened his first high street estate agency in Tavistock, Devon. After several years of selling properties via a website, he has just opened his first bricks-and-mortar shop in the hope of attracting more customers and making prospective purchasers feel more comfortable with the idea of buying property overseas.

He says that many people feel happier buying through a high street shop than via a website: 'The big problem with my industry is that everyone buys a property either over the phone or after falling in love with something while they are on holiday or at a property exhibition. They are often handing over a huge amount of money on the basis of a magazine advert and a conversation on the phone. Whereas this way people have somewhere to walk into and meet someone face to face. They can pop in for an informal chat on their way to Tesco's and there is no pressure.'

If the first shop goes well Barrasford plans to have a chain of 15 shops across the country within the next three years. He says: 'I want to build a brand. If people want to buy a television they may think of going to Dixons. If people want to buy an overseas property I want them to think of us.'

If you choose a business with scalability it also has enormous implications for the operating costs of your business. Ronen points out: 'The best opportunities are businesses that can grow without any significant increase in operating costs. Software producers, for example, can write a piece of software and once it is written it makes no difference whether they sell 1 or 50,000 units. That makes it a very scalable business because the marginal cost of the software is effectively close to zero.'

In addition, businesses that are easily scalable are likely to have fewer problems managing their size as they get bigger. If you have to write bespoke software every time you get a contract from a new customer, instead of having pre-written software that you can sell to anyone, then you will need to hire people to do the work each time you get a new contract. That can become extremely problematic, partly because it gets very expensive to hire people to work for you each time and partly because you will end up having to cope with lots of operational issues such as dealing with a fluid work force.

Even if you are not able to take advantage of your business's inherent scalability from day one, the important thing is that the potential is there for you to tap into at some point. Without it your business will be stuck in first gear – with it the sky is the limit.

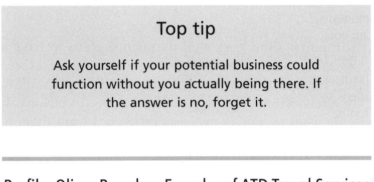

Top tip

Ask yourself if your potential business could function without you actually being there. If the answer is no, forget it.

Profile: Oliver Brendon, Founder of ATD Travel Services

For someone who is so good at making money, Oliver Brendon is surprisingly bad at managing it. Despite owning 100 per cent of a business that in 2008 is set to have a turnover of £38 million and has been profitable since year one, he still has not got round to paying off the mortgage on his home.

He says: 'I just stick all the money in the company. My auditors and my accountant think I am completely insane because the money is sitting in bonds and I haven't paid off my mortgage. But I am not interested in personal finance in the slightest.'

Born and brought up with an older brother in Cambridge, where his mother was a teacher and his father wrote books, Brendon spent all his spare time playing football. He dreamed of playing football professionally. But at the age of 14 he did work experience at Thomas Cook, the travel agents, and from that moment on he was hooked on the idea of working in the travel industry.

He says: 'That gave me more direction in life than anything I did at school because I had a glimpse of the kind of work I wanted to do. I looked up to their product managers and at the time it seemed very glamorous to be going to stay in hotels in far flung places.'

He ended up spending the next five years working for Thomas Cook during the school holidays. When he left school at 18 with two poor A levels he took an HND course in travel management at Durham and then a degree in travel at Newcastle University.

The inspiration for his future business came in 1997, in the third year of the course, when Brendon got a placement working as a holiday rep in Florida. His main job was to sell tickets to the big Florida theme parks such as Disneyworld, Universal Studios and Seaworld on commission.

He says: 'At the time people arriving by plane usually didn't have theme park tickets because they hadn't bought them in advance. It struck me that there was an opportunity to sell these tickets in advance in the UK rather than take a big chunk of people's spending money once they got there. The most expensive component of a Florida holiday is the theme park tickets. The average spend on them is around £850 for a family of four.'

After finishing his degree Brendon got a job in the UK office of the company he had worked for in Florida. He discovered that although the company was selling Florida theme park tickets to people in advance, they were only selling them through travel agents. However, he was not ready to pursue his plan and when the business went bankrupt he got a job with the Florida tourist board.

While he was there he made a lot of contacts in the industry but after four years the relentless bureaucracy of the organisation had started to wear him down and he resigned, aged 27. He says: 'It was run with public money so I would have to write a report to be able to buy some stationery. It stifled me because it was so uncommercial.'

By this time Brendon felt ready to start his own business selling theme park tickets direct to the public. He says: 'I had read that whatever you do in business you must know it, and the only thing I really knew inside out was buying and selling tickets.' The internet was in its infancy at the time, so he borrowed £10,000 from his father, rented a desk in an office and created a basic website to sell the tickets via the internet.

He says: 'I did a business plan and it had two absolute no's – I would never sell through a travel agent and I would never sell tickets for anything that got full, such as a hotel. The reason for that was it meant I could take bookings wherever I was, whether at home or in the car, because I knew there was unlimited availability.' By doing that Brendon had given his business the ultimate winning tool – it could be scaled up, to a potentially unlimited size.

His business was an instant success, with Brendon selling £3 million worth of tickets in the first year despite handling all the sales himself. In the second year, by now with two people helping him, he had sales of £10 million and in the third year a five-strong team pushed turnover to £24 million.

Brendon admits to making a number of mistakes along the way. The first has been to constantly buy foreign currency at a poor exchange rate. 'Every year I have bought currency badly', he says. 'If you could have picked the worst times to buy dollars, that is when I have bought them. When I finally do get one right we will make a lot more money.'

His second mistake has been his failure to find good offices for the business. 'I pick bad offices. In our first office the roof leaked and the wall caved in. As a result we have moved four times in five years, which is very stressful. I just make very impulsive and quick decisions. Sometimes that works very well but some decisions should be given a little bit more thought.'

But as the business has grown Brendon has been able to expand into selling tickets to theme parks in other parts of the United States such as New York and Las Vegas. In 2006 he also added another strand to the business by launching www.dosomethingdifferent.com, a website that sells tickets to attractions and activities throughout the world such as tickets to horse racing in Hong Kong and indoor skiing in Dubai. The site currently offers 650 events and activities but the ability of the business to scale up means that now the sky is the limit.

Now 32 and married with one child, Brendon has this advice for budding entrepreneurs: 'The best advice is probably not to listen to too much advice. When I set up my business there were some quite high profile people in the industry who told me I was mad and said it would never work. But if I had listened to them I would still be working at the Florida tourist board writing a report on why I needed to order some rulers. You have to go with your gut instinct.'

7

Protect your idea

You have a brilliant idea for a product and you have spent months out in the garden shed making a fantastic prototype out of brown paper and bits of string. You have never seen anything like it in the shops and are convinced it is just what the public has been waiting for.

There can be few more tantalising dreams than inventing something that makes your fortune. And few more alarming prospects than having someone steal your idea before you start.

If you think you have created a genuinely new product or process then the best way of protecting your invention is to get it patented. A patent gives inventors a monopoly on their products for up to 20 years by giving them the right to stop anyone else from making the product or using it without permission. If someone tries, you can take them to court.

Not only does the patent establish the invention or process as being yours, it also means it can be bought, sold, rented or licensed. That means it can be a useful bargaining tool when trying to persuade manufacturers and investors to get on board.

Richard Burton, Innovation Adviser at Business Link for London, says: 'To the inventor the advantage of a patent is it gives them some sort of edge when it comes to negotiating with a company that is going to buy the idea. It says there is some value in it.'

Your first step is to make sure nobody has thought of your idea already. You can do that by visiting the website of the UK Intellectual Property Office, formerly known as The Patent Office (www.ipo.gov.uk). It lists 30 million patents worldwide and contains advice on how to access the details. If you still think your idea is unique you can apply for a patent from the UK Intellectual Property Office by filing a description and submitting drawings.

If your application is in any way complicated, you should get a patent attorney to advise you. This can be expensive, but there are ways round it. Ron Hamilton, an entrepreneur who developed a manufacturing process that enabled him to make disposable contact lenses, could not afford to go through the patent process himself. So he entered into an agreement with British Technology Group, which markets bright ideas from academia, in which he assigned the patent to them in return for 50 per cent of the ensuing income. Once the patent was granted Hamilton was able to get additional investment. Within three years he was able to sell the business, including the intellectual property, to the eyewear company Bausch & Lomb for £33 million.

He says: 'Patents are central to creating value in a business. You can develop the business without a patent but it will be valueless because it can be replicated. You must give yourself a competitive advantage and to do that you must look at every aspect of protecting your intellectual property.'

But what if your idea is a product or service that is simply an improvement on something that exists and so could not be protected by patent? The first step is to see what elements of it you can still protect. You may be able to register trademarks and design rights with the UK Intellectual Property Office – you can find details on their website.

The next step is to draw up a simple confidentiality agreement which you ask interested parties to sign before revealing details of your business idea. Giles Crown, a partner at the law firm Lewis Silkin, says a confidentiality agreement should be short (an A4 sheet of paper), basic and preferably drawn up by a lawyer. He says: 'It should define what information you are talking about, and state that both parties will agree to keep it confidential and will use it only for the purposes of the particular discussion that they are having.'

However Crown says that while confidentiality agreements can be useful, in reality budding entrepreneurs may struggle to get people to sign them. 'The difficulty tends to be that the people you are talking to are in a position of power and won't sign it. Or they will send it to their legal department and it will take ages and everything just gets bogged down.'

If you find yourself in this situation, he says, the best thing to do is make clear in all correspondence that the information you discussed is confidential. 'Head your correspondence "strictly confidential" and put in your letters that you are sharing this on a confidential basis. If there is a presentation put "strictly confidential, all rights reserved" on it and the copyright sign with your name and the year. You can still have a confidential relationship even if there isn't a written agreement.'

Another way of establishing the date you came up with an idea is to send details of the idea in a sealed envelope, either to yourself or to a lawyer. The postmark, which can be placed over the seal, will prove that you thought of your invention before that date.

However it is important to get fears about someone stealing your idea into proportion. Harry Cragoe is the founder of PJ Smoothies, which makes drinks from blended fruit, and which he sold in 2005 for £20 million.

He says that even if people think your idea is a good one and worth pursuing they are highly unlikely to do anything about it. 'I have lost count of the number of people I have met who said what a good idea mine was and that they had been thinking of doing it themselves. The world is full of people who are thinking of doing something – there aren't very many who get off their backsides and do it.'

He adds that even if someone did actually try to copy his idea they would have been at a significant disadvantage: 'Unless someone had been working on it for some time I knew I was at least two years ahead of them. I also arrogantly thought that I could do it better than anyone else.'

In the event, says Cragoe, it took four years for a rival to launch a competing smoothie product on the market.

Certainly, the fear of someone stealing your idea should not deter you from telling relevant people – such as advisers, accountants and solicitors – about your plans, because otherwise they will not be able to help you. As Steve Clark, Chief Executive of Entrust, a local enterprise agency covering northeast England, says: 'It is vitally important that you run your ideas past people who have some expertise otherwise you will just be punting into isolation and will have no real idea whether the thing is going to be a success or a turkey. Anything that reduces business risk has to be a good thing and discussing and sharing is an integral part of that process.'

Top tip

Keep a record of who you talk to about your idea
and when the conversation took place.

Profile: Laura Tenison, founder of JoJo Maman Bebe

When Laura Tenison decided to start her own clothes-making business she had one small problem. Manufacturing would require a substantial amount of start-up capital but, at 22, she had no money.

Instead of giving up her dream though she initially decided to open a service business, which would require only minimal capital and allow her to build up the capital she needed. So when a friend enlisted her to help her buy a house in France Tenison spotted an opportunity to set up a property agency there. She says: 'The overseas property markets were opening up and I realised there was a huge gap in the market for a good agency'.

She found out how to become an agent in France and in 1992 set up a property agency that also handled renovations and lettings, using £3,000 borrowed from one of her brothers. She ran it from her bedroom in the flat she shared in the UK and commuted to France every second weekend.

Two and a half years later she managed to sell the agency for £70,000. It was time to start her clothing business.

Tenison first discovered her love of making clothes as a child when her parents bought her a sewing machine at the age of 12. Although the youngest of five children, she spent much of her childhood alone in Pontypool, South Wales, because her siblings were at boarding school. So she was forced to find ways of entertaining herself. She says: 'That sewing machine was my constant companion'.

She soon moved on to making clothes for other people. By the age of 15, while still at school, she was making and selling silk garments for men for weddings and special occasions. 'I always had an entrepreneurial spirit', she says.

None of her family took her clothes-making seriously however and when she left school her father decided she should become a bilingual secretary. Tenison says: 'It was always considered a hobby. No one suggested that I should go to art school or do a fashion design degree. It was really just a way of keeping me quiet'.

However she continued to make and sell clothes in her spare time. After six months spent working in a technical publishing company and two years spent travelling she decided to create an apprenticeship for herself in the clothing industry. She wrote to every manufacturer in the phone book that was also a retailer and was eventually offered a job at Aquascutum, where she spent 18 months learning about buying and retailing.

Setting up the French property agency followed. But just as she sold it to start up her clothes business Tenison was involved in a serious car crash. She ended up in hospital with broken bones and had to stay there for several weeks.

Tenison had planned to make men's clothes when she started up her business but while she was in hospital she got talking to the lady in the next bed who was trying to buy clothes for her children from mail order catalogues. The lady was not having much success finding anything she liked and suggested that Tenison make children's clothes instead.

Tenison was intrigued by the idea. As soon as she was discharged from hospital she did some market research by standing outside Mothercare on London's Oxford Street handing out questionnaires. On the strength of the replies she decided to sell maternity and children's wear via mail order.

She found a Colombian factory that was prepared to make her designs in small quantities and stored her stock in a garage belonging to one of her brothers. Then Tenison immediately grabbed the attention of the press with the launch of a bright pink maternity catsuit. 'It wasn't a best-seller but it got us a lot of PR', she says.

After two years however she faced disaster when the pound devalued. She had to remortgage her house to keep the business afloat.

Two years later there was another crisis. She had initially called the business JoJo. But although she had registered it as a company name she had not registered it as a trade name. As a result she had not sufficiently protected her idea and so another company with a similar name sued her for 'passing off'. In the end it cost Tenison £25,000 to fight it and she had to agree to call the business JoJo Maman Bebe in future. 'It was a lesson to be learnt', she says.

She opened her first shop in 2004 in Battersea. Initially she thought she would need an outside investor to enable her to open more shops. But after six months of talking to private-equity firms she realised that the company could probably go it alone and fund the shops from internal growth.

'With no outside investors there is no pressure', she says. It meant that when Tenison had problems with a couple of new stores she was able to slow down her expansion programme until the stores were on track. 'Outside investors might have said: "You were going to open eight shops a year – so open eight shops a year".'

Today JoJo Maman Bebe has 30 stores in the UK and is in the process of opening stores in Italy. Turnover in 2008 is expected to be £18 million.

Now 41 and married with two children, Tenison still owns 99.25 per cent of the business, having given 0.75 per cent to a former employee. She has been awarded an MBE for services to businesses in Wales where her factories are based and thinks the secret of her success is having a huge amount of energy: 'I never like to stand still'.

She has this advice for budding entrepreneurs: 'Don't ever give up. Start as young as you can because you will be much more brave. You have to take risks but make sure those risks are calculated. Keep control while delegating. And pay attention to detail'.

8

Make sure the numbers add up

So you have found your brilliant idea, you have researched your market and you are convinced your business is going to be a winner. Now get a blank piece of paper and a pen, close the door and sit down in a quiet room. It is time to start trying to get your numbers to add up.

One of the most common reasons why start-up businesses fail is because they run out of money before they are able to get to a point where the business is able to sustain itself independently from the money it generates from sales of its product or service. In fact some would-be businesses never even get as far as actually being launched and in a position to start selling because the entrepreneur runs out of money before they are able to develop it sufficiently to get it to that stage. Imagine how galling that would be. You have gone to all the effort of having a good idea and spending months researching your market. Then in the end customers never even get a chance to try your product or service because the cash runs out before you are able to get it to market.

The solution is to get the numbers right before you even embark on your business venture. Start with the basics. How much will it cost to make your product? Will the cost fall as you make more units? Will it be cheaper to make them yourself or to get someone else to make them? How much will you be able to sell them for? If you are going to be supplying your product to a shop rather than direct to customers, how much will they be able to sell it for? How many do you think you will be able to sell in a week? What about the cost of packaging, storage and transport? What about the cost of hiring staff?

As you can see, as soon as you embark on this exercise the questions will come thick and fast as you delve deeper and deeper into what shape your business will take.

Of course once you have got the hang of it you can progress to working out your cash flow, turnover and profit projections and so on. But the key, especially if numbers are not your strong point, is to take it one step at a time so you do not get overwhelmed and give up. For most would-be entrepreneurs the idea of having to sit down and add up numbers is a really horrible thought and it is extremely tempting to convince yourself that you will somehow be able to wing it and make it up as you go along. It is also inevitably a slightly surreal exercise as you will have to start thinking about such things as how many products you are likely to be selling in three years' time when you have yet to sell a single one. But you must force yourself to do it. Even if your numbers at this stage are largely a combination of guesstimates and wishful thinking, just the act of thinking about all this stuff and writing it down will help clarify what exactly it is that you are trying to achieve with your business and where you hope it will be in two, five or ten years. It will also give you, and other people, confidence that you actually know what you are talking about and really can make it work.

More than that, without a business plan – for that is what you are effectively creating by doing this – you have little chance of getting a bank, venture capitalist or anyone else to lend you money. Or of getting advice and support from a government agency such as Business Link. If you have ever watched an episode of *Dragons' Den* on BBC television, where budding entrepreneurs have to persuade a panel of successful entrepreneurs to invest in their product, then you will know just how important figures are – and how important it is that you know them inside out.

Barry Franklin, a business adviser with Business Link for London, says: 'It may be tedious to do all the research, budgets and forecasting, but the fact is that without a proper business plan you really don't know if your idea is going to work. It is like the old saying, if you don't know where you are going, you are never going to get there. The main causes of business failure are lack of planning, lack of money, lack of appropriate skills and reluctance to take advice. Failing to plan is planning to fail.'

Along with your numbers – which should also include how much money you will raise, what it will be used for and how and when you intend to pay it back – your business plan should include an explanation of what you are aiming to do and how you intend to go about it. You should aim for 12 pages of clear, concise information, typed on one side only and well laid out so it is easy to read. If an empty computer screen or blank sheet of paper is too daunting for you to get started, talk your plan into a tape recorder and transcribe it.

Linda Marie Kerr opened her Funsters Fun Factory, an indoor adventure playground for children, in 2003, 11 years after she dreamt up the idea. She raised the £150,000 needed to start the business in Hendy, South Wales, by borrowing £80,000 from her husband and getting a £70,000 loan from NatWest.

Kerr got the bank loan after presenting the bank manager with a six-page business plan. 'I thought that writing it was going to be a long arduous task – and it was', she says. 'It took from March to September to get all the information. I found the projections really hard. It was difficult to make forecasts for something I hadn't even started; I didn't want to be over-confident, but I didn't want to undersell myself either. One week I thought: "This is ridiculous", and screwed up the plan and threw it in the bin.'

But Kerr knew that the bank had to be able to visualise what she was doing. So she tried again and eventually put together an information pack with an outline of what the business was and her aims for it. 'Now the plan has become my bible', she says. 'It has given me monthly targets that I would probably not have thought about.'

It is worth reminding yourself from time to time that your figures, and your business plan as a whole, are not set in stone. You cannot hope to get them right first time. And as you learn more about what you are doing and start to tell people about it, new ideas and opportunities and different ways of doing things will present themselves. These will need to be incorporated into the outline you have already drawn up. A business plan is very much a work in progress.

Top tip

Do not underestimate the amount of money you will need. Work out a figure and then double it. You are likely to be nearer the mark.

Profile: Loyd Hitchmough, founder of Cheshire Cookers

The first time Loyd Hitchmough tried his hand at reconditioning an Aga cooker was nearly his last. After buying the cooker it took him eight hours to get it out of its owner's kitchen, something that should have taken less than an hour.

'If I hadn't paid the guy in advance I would have just walked away. It was that difficult', he says. 'I thought: "Bloody hell, what have I done here?". But I just persevered with it and at the end of the day the Aga was in the back of my van.'

It was worth the effort. His company, Cheshire Cookers, now sells 600 reconditioned Aga cookers a year and in 2008 will have a turnover of £3 million.

Hitchmough was born and brought up in Manchester where his father ran his own used-car business. At first, he was not interested in going into business himself. An only child, he was keen on music and learnt to play the piano and clarinet at a young age. He was good at them and after leaving school went to music college.

His other big interest was canal boats and while he was at college he lived for two years on an old slipper launch that he had bought and restored.

After three years at college, however, Hitchmough realised he was not interested in becoming a professional musician. 'I wanted to get a job and start earning money', he says. 'All my friends had jobs and money to spend and I felt as though I was missing out. I wanted to be buying clothes and going to the pub like everybody else.'

So after graduating from music college he had a complete change of lifestyle. He sold the boat and got a job with the gas board as an administrator processing bills. 'I regretted letting the boat go but I have no regrets at all about letting the music go. It was just a stage in my life', he says.

After 12 months with the gas board Hitchmough got a job selling cars, like his father, and ended up spending 15 years in the industry, eventually becoming a general manager for Honda. He says: 'Sales was something that came quite naturally to me.'

Hitchmough often toyed with the idea of starting his own business but never got very far. 'I had been to the bank a few times with a few business plans. They were generally motor-trade related, like windscreen repairs, bumper repairs, that sort of thing. But I wasn't able to make them work and I didn't get the support of the bank.'

Then, in 1996, at the age of 35, he and his wife bought a converted barn in Cheshire and decided that what it really needed in the kitchen was a traditional Aga cooker. He says: 'It was crying out for an Aga but we didn't have enough money to go out and buy a new one. So we went on the hunt for a second-hand one.'

They found it difficult to track down a reconditioned Aga but that gave Hitchmough an idea. 'It was a very sleepy industry and I thought there could be a niche in the market providing reconditioned Aga cookers.' This time he was so convinced he was on to a winner he did not even bother drawing up a business plan or talking to his bank manager. 'I had £800 in my pocket and so I went out and bought an old Aga', he says.

After teaching himself how to strip it down and repair it so it looked and performed like a new cooker, Hitchmough sold it and with the money he made bought another old Aga to recondition. He taught himself everything he knew. 'A lot of it is common sense', he says. 'I learnt from my mistakes and made sure that I didn't make those mistakes again.'

He put an advertisement in the local paper that brought in both old cookers and people wishing to buy reconditioned ones. 'People were phoning me to sell Agas and also to buy Agas. The two formed a magic circle.' At the time, in 1996, he was buying them for about £1,000 and selling them for just over double that. For his customers, his reconditioned Agas were still a good buy – new Agas sell for more than £10,000. In other words Hitchmough had ensured the one crucial element of any successful business – he had made sure the numbers added up.

By this stage he was going all over the country to collect old Agas from people's houses and then working through the night to repair them. It was at this point that he decided to give up his car job and concentrate on developing his fledgling business full time. He says: 'My wife was studying for a degree and we had just had another baby so it was a bit of a critical time. But I thought I'd grab the bull by the horns and go for it.'

Without any external investment, however, it was hard going. 'I had to make sure I sold one Aga to buy the next one and that continued for about two years, living hand to mouth. I would be in Scotland one day and the Isle of Wight the next. It was hard work but it was worth it because I was enjoying it and meeting some incredible people.'

After three years Hitchmough was earning enough money to be able to hire an engineer to help him, training him up himself. He has also spent £2 million on a new showroom for Cheshire Cookers, which will also enable him to sell kitchens alongside his Agas. Now 46, Hitchmough thinks the secret of his success has been to keep tight control of the company, of which he still owns 100 per cent.

'My philosophy has always been to start low and grow – to expand when we need to, and when we have the money', he says.

'Our company has benefited from that because I have not got any shareholders breathing down my neck telling me to move in a different direction or to liquidate stock to release capital. We can change direction at any point and if it doesn't work we can just go back to the drawing board. We are masters of our own destiny.'

9

Get your timing right

If you had asked a venture capitalist to invest in your fledgling internet business in 1999 at the height of the dotcom boom it is highly likely they would have welcomed you with open arms and started throwing vast sums of money at you. If you had waited until a year later when the boom had turned to bust, however, it is unlikely you would even have had your phone calls returned.

Timing can play an enormous part in determining whether a business is a success – or even whether it is able to get off the ground in the first place. So how do you go about improving your chances of getting it right?

The first thing to realise is that there are some things you cannot do anything about. The weather being one of them. Snap elections called by politicians being another. But there are other aspects of timing that you can control.

The first thing you need to do is find out everything you can about the market you are going to be launching your product or service into and make sure you know it inside out. Is there some forthcoming legislation that is going to shift market demand? Is there a global trend that is having a big impact on what new products and services are being produced, and what segments of consumers are being enticed into the market? If you can find out what other people are doing then it will give you a good idea of what you should be doing too. In 2007, for example, one of the biggest driving forces in the market was for 'green' products and services that had a beneficial environmental impact. But in five years time, it could be something else entirely, and in ten years something completely different again.

While entering a market too early has its own challenges – not least the fact that you may end up having to explain to everyone what your product does and why people suddenly need it in their lives when they did not before – the one thing you definitely do not want to do is enter it too late. Because doing that you will discover little or no demand for your product as everyone else has got there first.

Doug Richard, a former judge on the BBC television show *Dragons' Den* and Chairman of Library House, which provides research on private fast-growth companies, says: 'If you go into an opportunity and find you are the tenth person in then you should really ask yourself, what is it about me that is so special? Because you can't just be only a bit better than someone else who is doing something similar – you have to be remarkably better.'

David Lewis, who runs a marketing consultancy called The Mindlab, says that in order to get your timing right you need to work out what your potential customers are thinking. And in order to do that you need to do what they do. That means reading the same magazines, joining the same clubs and visiting the same places, whether that is art-school exhibitions or clubs in Ibiza.

He says: 'The secret of success is to find out exactly what is going on in the marketplace. You can't do it from behind a desk – you need to get out there and listen to what people are saying. Big companies employ people called "cool hunters" to find out what is going on. If a company makes trendy clothes for young people, for example, the cool hunter will go round the clubs that young people go to and see what is being worn. Entrepreneurs have to be their own cool hunters.'

Clare Brynteson got her timing spot on when she founded Buy Time, a lifestyle management service for businesses and individuals (www.buy-time.co.uk). A former high flier at investment bank Goldman Sachs, she launched the business, which provides customers with a personal assistant on an hourly basis to do everything from organising a parking permit to getting broadband connected, after realising that a growing number of people like her just did not have time to do simple every-day tasks in their lives and would be prepared to pay someone else to do them.

She says: 'It was blindingly obvious to me that the timing was right to do this because I could see that people around me were suffering from a lack of time and really needed this service. With women increasingly working the same hours as men there was no one at home to take care of anything.'

Even more important than the lack of time, she says, was that people were increasingly prepared to pay for outside help. 'A few years previously people would have just laughed at the idea and thought how ridiculous it was to have a personal assistant for your personal life. The key was putting the service in front of people at a time when they absolutely needed it rather than when they were question-ing whether they needed it.' Brynteson now has 12 staff working for her and 300 clients.

Of course getting your timing right is not just about getting right the timing of your product or service hitting the marketplace, it is also about getting your own personal timing right. Moving house, coping with illness and having a baby, for example, are three events that are not necessarily conducive to starting up a business. It can be done, but if you have a choice you might prefer to wait until there is less going on at home before you commit to spending 24 hours a day building up a business.

You should also make sure you are launching only when you have sufficient knowledge of what you are doing. Keith Hunt, managing partner at business advisers Results International, says: 'If you have worked in a big corporate all your life but you have long had a dream to open a restaurant don't start it until you have learnt the trade inside out. Get a job in the business even if it is lowly paid and work out how it all ticks.'

Another important aspect to consider is your own feelings. If you are absolutely desperate to be your own boss and cannot bear to wait any longer then that can be as important as external factors in determining whether the time is right. As Mark Riminton, a director of Shirlaws, a business-coaching company puts it: 'Starting up a business requires a huge amount of commitment and has a huge effect on people's lives – so the most important thing is that you actually want to do it. You can have the best idea in the world and the best commercial opportunity but if you don't have the will and the commitment to follow it through it is not going to go anywhere.'

Having said all that, the one thing you should try to avoid is becoming too obsessed with whether your timing is right or not. If you waited for everything to be perfect then you would probably never actually start a business.

Top tip

The first person may get all the attention but it is usually the second person going into a market who makes all the money.

Profile: Jan Smith, founder of EOL IT Services

Jan Smith was always competitive even as a child. Born and brought up in Essex, where her father worked for the Port of London Authority, she was one of four children and a bit of a tomboy.

'My mother always described me as the cheeky one', she says. 'When I was a child I had more friends who were boys because I enjoyed the challenge of boys' activities – marbles, cycling, climbing trees and the general competitiveness.'

Her first childhood challenge, however, was to overcome a serious speech impediment that she thinks was caused by the trauma of experiencing a bad fire at the family home. 'I went to speech therapy for four years and really struggled to put one word in front of the other', she says.

After leaving school at 16, Smith briefly worked in a bank and then for a solicitor before giving up employment to marry and have children. But she continued to do casual work from home, holding parties to sell children's clothes and Christmas decorations. 'I was always chomping at the bit to do other things', she says.

So at 29, when her elder son was eight, Smith got a job working for a small company that compiled databases for the British School of Motoring. She started to learn everything she could about information technology, being promoted through the industry until she became a sales manager.

'I was quite ambitious and had a lot of determination', she says. 'I think when you've had a humble upbringing you either decide that is your lot in life and you should accept it or you aspire to do other things. I always felt I wanted to do better.'

But in 1989, when she was 40, Smith was unexpectedly made redundant. 'I sat down for a while and thought there's no need to worry, someone will call and offer me a job', she says. 'But the phone didn't ring.'

She decided to start an IT company of her own. But after three years it failed and she put the firm into liquidation. Although she then found work as an IT consultant she still dreamt of running her own company again. In 1996, she realised there might be a gap in the market for a firm that disposed of old and unwanted computer equipment.

She says: 'When I was working in the IT industry I was always involved in supplying new products but what concerned me was seeing all the old equipment being chucked into a skip. It seemed a tremendous shame that it was just going to waste.'

Her solution was to start End-O-Line, an IT asset-recycling company now renamed EOL IT Services. Her timing could not have been better. Smith started by going into large firms and offering to take away their unwanted equipment such as monitors, PCs, printers and photocopiers that had ceased to be of any use to the company. She would do a complete audit of the items she took away and if a piece of equipment still had some value she would pay the company for it. If not, the company would pay her to take it away. She and her partner, who was initially involved in the business with her, would then either refurbish the equipment to resell or recycle the parts.

She says: 'Sometimes we would bring the equipment back and it would not have any memory or hard drive. So we would put a hard drive and memory into it which would enable us to sell it on as a refurbished unit.'

Her first client was JP Morgan and, as word of her recycling services spread, Smith started taking on more corporate clients. In the past couple of years EOL IT services has received a big boost for its services with the introduction of the EU's Waste Electrical and Electronic Equipment (WEEE) directive. This directive came into effect in 2007 and has forced companies to dispose of their old IT equipment responsibly.

Smith has made sure that the recycling ethos continues through the company. She says: 'We have a zero-landfill policy, which means that 90 per cent of everything we buy in or collect goes back into the marketplace in either complete or component form. The remaining 10 per cent is recycled. None of it goes into landfill.'

She has since bought out her former partner's share of the business and now has six members of her family working for her, including her elder son, who is an engineer, and her sister, who is company secretary. The business, based in Maldon, Essex, now has 42 staff and is expected to have a turnover in 2008 of £3.2 million.

Smith, now 59, says the secret of success is to believe in yourself. She says: 'My philosophy in life is really just to go for it and prove that you can do things and not be put down by your own self-doubt. I have always believed that if I walk in a straight line I will achieve what I want to achieve.

'I've always been an extremely hard-working person and I always will be. Sometimes my sons ask me when I'm going to retire, and I say: "When I'm 90".'

10

Test your commitment

When Sarah Manby found it impossible to find a nice dog collar for her dog Murphy, it inspired her to start up her own online business, Mango Mutt, selling natural and organic accessories for dogs (www.mangomutt.co.uk). Being passionate about dogs herself, she realised she did not want Mango Mutt simply to be another anonymous website selling products. So she started replying individually to every customer's email, asking them how their dogs were getting on. She also started up a forum for dog owners on the site, inviting new customers to send in a photo of their dog to put up on the website so that people visiting the site could vote for their favourite dog each month. The winner receives a bag of organic handmade dog biscuits – which Manby bakes herself at home. She also regularly walks her dog with local customers and their dogs.

There is no such thing as a half-hearted entrepreneur. Successful entrepreneurs do not use sentences that begin with the words 'I don't really mind about…' or 'I can't be bothered to…' or 'Let's do it next week…'.

Instead they use words like passion and drive and even obsession. They will happily talk about their product or service for hours, to anyone who will listen. Then they will pore over competitors' websites in excruciating detail, drive for hours simply to show you the spot where their new factory will be built, and make you stay up all night tasting their latest products and making notes.

This is not coincidence. The fact is that in order to succeed at something that has such a high failure rate – two-thirds of all business start-ups fail within the first three years – you have to have more than just a vague desire to give it a go. You have to have a deep burning need to make it work, one that will not go away no matter how hard you try to ignore it.

Becoming a successful entrepreneur is hard work. It is not something that you can do with half an eye on other things. So you really need to be sure that this is what you want to do more than anything else in the world in order to stand any chance of making it a success.

Fraser Mackay, Small Business Marketing Director at Barclays Bank, says: 'A lot of small business customers work very long hours in the early days setting their business up. It can be a thankless task and if you are not the sort of person who has the time or the commitment to do that you really should be asking yourself whether it's for you.'

Having a passion for what you are trying to do is important not just to sustain you through the long dark nights alone in the office or the months of lost sleep. It is also vital in getting other people on board too. Enthusiasm is infectious. If you believe 100 per cent in what you are doing, then you stand a much better chance of being able to persuade other people – family, friends, investors, customers, bank managers or employees – to believe in it too.

So how do you know if you have a strong enough desire to start up your own business? It may seem like a tempting idea compared to the drudgery of your nine to five job, but do you really have enough commitment to see it through? One way to find out is to try it out for yourself. If you want to open a restaurant, get a job as a waiter or dishwasher at evenings and weekends. If you want to make and sell jam, make a batch and take a stall at your local farmers' market or village fete and see how you get on. It will not take long for you to discover whether you are loving the experience or hating it. And before you protest that these are lowly jobs and bear no resemblance to being the boss of your own firm, remember that if you do start up your own business you will undoubtedly end up doing all the horrible jobs at one time or another, from cleaning the toilets to unblocking the drains. It comes with the territory.

Of course one of the main reasons why people start up their own business is for the tantalising prospect of being able to sell it one day for an enormous amount of money. And undoubtedly there are some people for whom the prospect of becoming rich is the only motivation they need. But for many other people pursuing that sole financial goal is simply not enough to carry them through all the way to the other side. If you do not have a real enthusiasm for what you are doing to accompany that desire to make money then it is likely you will stumble. That is because at some point the prospect of making all the money in the world will not seem enough to compensate for the months of lost sleep, the lack of any social life, the loneliness and isolation of sitting in a room by yourself for months on end, and of the small but important things like missing your partner's birthday or not being able to attend your child's school play. In these situations passion is not just an advantage; it is the life force that will keep you going.

Not only that, if you are doing it purely for the money then at some point you are likely to become impatient because the pot of gold never seems to get any closer and you will start to make bad decisions. You will fail to invest in long-term growth, whether that is in people, equipment or customer service. You will make do and mend where you should be thinking big.

One of the best ways to deal with this is to find something in your life that you already feel passionate about and then turn it into a successful business. Like Sarah Manby, you could base your business around a hobby or pastime. If you love skiing, for example, you might think about starting up a ski holiday business. Or if you enjoy looking after children you might think about opening a chain of nurseries.

Then again you might find your idea from pursuing a cause you care about deeply, such as making organic food for children or developing biodegradable plastic bottles. Increasingly many successful entrepreneurs are using their skills not just to create a profitable business but in some small way to change the world for the better. It is possible to make a profit and do good. And if you are passionate about getting your product or service out into the market where it can benefit others then there is no greater motivation to make a business work.

Above all, choose something that you enjoy doing because for the first few years at least you are going to be doing a very great deal of it. Energy, enthusiasm, commitment, drive, determination, passion. Not just for a few weeks but for years and years and years. It sounds exhausting and it is. Then again, if it was easy everyone would do it.

Top tip

Do not follow the money. If you are any good at what you are doing then it will follow you.

Profile: Annabel Karmel, founder of Annabel Karmel group

Anyone who has a young child is likely to have heard of Annabel Karmel as her recipe books for babies and toddlers have sold in their millions. But before she became interested in children's food and nutrition Karmel pursued a very different career. Having begun to play the harp at seven she studied at the Royal College of Music after leaving school and followed a successful career as a professional musician, recording albums, appearing on television and performing around the world.

'I really enjoyed what I was doing', she says. 'I played Cinderella with a harp in pantomime with Dennis Waterman and played on television with Bruce Forsyth and Dick Emery.'

She continued her musical career after she got married at the age of 24. When she was 27, however, her first child Natasha died at the age of three months of a viral infection. 'It was just devastating. I couldn't believe it could happen. My whole life fell apart. I couldn't play music. I felt it was somehow superficial. I cancelled my engagements and wandered round like a zombie', she says.

Karmel had another child, Nicholas. But when he refused to eat properly as a toddler she realised she wanted to do something about it. 'Being a mum with a child who had died and one who wouldn't eat made me very vulnerable', she says. 'I was determined that he would eat well.'

She had already started a playgroup near her home in north London and began to create recipes for food that she hoped her son would eat, giving them to other mothers to try as well. The recipes got an enthusiastic response so Karmel decided to write a cookery book about feeding children.

She says: 'I didn't know anything about it. I didn't even know how to type. But I thought it would be good therapy – a way of getting over Natasha's death.' She spent the next two and a half years doing research into child nutrition and creating recipes to test on the children at the playgroup without having any idea whether her book would ever be published. It was a real test of her commitment to the project but she never thought of giving up.

It was in many ways a typical response by Karmel. Born and brought up in London with her brother by parents who both worked, her father as a manufacturer of shoe soles and her mother as an architect, Karmel had learnt a strong work ethic from an early age. 'I was made to work hard. My mother always believed that girls should have a career', she says.

When the book was finished she sent it to 15 publishers and every one of them rejected it. Fortunately at this point Karmel's luck changed. She discovered that someone she played tennis with was going to the Frankfurt Book Fair where many publishing deals are done. Her tennis partner offered to take her manuscript with him and on his return told her that the publisher Simon & Schuster wanted to take it on.

The Complete Baby and Toddler Meal Planner was published in 1991 and has since sold more than two million copies, making it one of the best selling cookery books in Britain. 'You do need luck. But you should never give up', says Karmel, who has now written 14 books about feeding youngsters, including *Superfoods for Babies and Children*.

She was also asked by Boots to design a range of cookery equipment, such as blenders and pots, to help parents feed their children. The range sold well and Karmel started thinking about creating her own range of ready-prepared meals for babies and children.

To begin with she was unsure how to go about it. She says: 'I was approached by a lot of very large companies to work with them and I think I lost time by talking to them. Eventually I realised that to begin with it would be better to do it by myself because I wanted to be in control of what I was doing.'

She hired a food consultant to help her find a factory that would make the products and invested £350,000 of her book royalties developing and testing the range. Her Eat Fussy range was launched in 2007 and is now stocked by Sainsbury's and Ocado. Total turnover from her books, meals and equipment is expected to be £14 million in 2008.

Now aged 48 and married with three children, Karmel thinks the secret of success is to believe in yourself. 'If you have a vision you have to trust yourself. Don't let other people put you off. And don't be worried about doing something by yourself', she says.

'I was worried about doing a food range by myself. I thought I had to have a big company behind me but actually it has been OK doing it by myself and very rewarding. Sometimes you think that everyone else is an expert and not you, but if you have a passion then go with it.'

However she admits to putting in very long hours to achieve that vision. She says: 'I regularly stay up until 3 am just to finish something off. I don't sleep much and I usually work the whole weekend. I gave up my social life for several years.'

Recently awarded an MBE for services to child nutrition, Karmel says she is driven by the need for security, something she thinks comes from seeing her mother have to take over as the family breadwinner when her father's business failed. She says: 'I have seen with my own parents how not having security affects the kids and the whole family unit. I have always wanted to make sure I have my own security because nobody can ever take that away from you. I don't want to be a multimillionaire but I do want to know that I will always have a roof over my head and will always be able to put food on the table. You should never rely on anyone but yourself.'

11

Learn to love technology

If you are a staunch Luddite or closet technophobe then this chapter is going to make you weep. But the fact is that no matter what kind of business you want to start up, whether it is a catering business or a chain of dog kennels, these days you are going to have to make use of every kind of technology available if your business has any chance of becoming a success.

Embracing technology means having a clear, easy-to-use website where customers can buy online if appropriate, and sending out regular e-mails to customers, perhaps in the form of a newsletter. It means having a state-of-the-art call queuing answerphone system for customers who ring up, perhaps with a ring back facility where customers can leave a message and still keep their place in the queue. It means providing yourself and any employees with mobile phones and Blackberries, and making sure your drivers have GPS navigation systems. It also means using up-to-date computer software systems for stock ordering and creating invoices. And it means thinking about how such things as webcams and parcel tracking software can make your business go faster and further than it could otherwise have done.

Apart from your own technological needs, you will need to consider the requirements that your customers and suppliers may place on you – for example, if you plan to supply a supermarket you are likely to need to barcode and date stamp your products.

It is no use protesting that because you are only a small business you are exempt from all of the above. It is tempting to think that because you are a small business you can act in a small way. But if your competitors are using the latest technology then you need to as well or you will go out of business. Size has got nothing to do with it. The fact is that having an efficient phone system and a user-friendly website will make the difference between a customer bothering to contact you or not.

The good news for you is that because you are just starting up a business you can incorporate the technology into your business structure right from the start. For longer-established businesses, bolting on new technology can be a lot harder to do and involve considerable pain during the transition period. And if you really do not know one end of a computer from the other there are lots of free courses available to help you – the government-backed Learn Direct (www.learndirect.co.uk) is a good place to start – and lots of IT companies you can employ if you need to.

The other piece of good news is that adopting technology does not have to cost a lot of money and yet can have a huge impact on whether a customer chooses to come to you or goes elsewhere. Think of the dog kennel business mentioned at the start of this chapter. If that were your business then with technology you can take bookings over the internet and allow customers to choose a menu and choice of activities for their animal during its stay. You can provide each owner with a daily e-mail describing what their pet has done that day. You can even enable customers to look at their animals via webcam from anywhere in the world to reassure themselves they are being well looked after. All of which sounds a lot more appealing than a dog kennel business where you are lucky if someone even bothers to answer the phone.

The stark fact is that all this new technology has not only provided new ways for businesses to become more efficient and new mediums for them to advertise in. It has also radically raised customers' expectations about the service they expect to receive from the businesses they buy from. And that means that every business, whether big or small, has to raise its game in order to be able to compete. For example, where once customers would have been content simply to order a product over the phone or by post and wait for it to arrive, they now want to be able to track its progress online from the warehouse to their door.

Of course one benefit of this explosion in technological capability for you, the budding entrepreneur, is that it has levelled the playing field for small start-ups by doing away with the need for expensive overheads like shops and offices. In fact, as many people are fast discovering, the internet can be the ideal way to start up a small business because it is quicker, cheaper and less bureaucratic than starting a bricks-and-mortar company.

Peter Crawshaw and Hugh Salmon are typical of the new-style entrepreneurs. They had the idea for their book-promotion business, Love reading (www.loveread ing.co.uk), while working in advertising. But instead of spending a fortune opening an office and recruiting staff as they might have done ten years ago, they spent just £10,000 building a basic website and researching the market.

Crawshaw says: 'We had an idea that we might be able to improve publisher relationships with readers and that morphed into the idea of Lovereading.co.uk, where readers can get extracts and publishers can promote their books.' More than 100,000 people have now registered to use the site and a business angel investor has invested £250,000 in the venture.

Crawshaw says there are several benefits to setting up online. 'The huge advantage is that you are able to test what you do at a lower risk. You don't have to invest in property and long leases', he says. 'Being online rather than on the high street is great because you can change and develop your service. In the first six months we were able to watch what our first customers did on the site, which helped to improve and develop the product.'

Another benefit to setting up an online company is that it makes it easy to measure the effectiveness of any web-based advertising of your product or service that you do. Devices such as Google's pay-per-click, for example, record exactly how many people are interested enough in your product to click on an icon in order to find out more. This means that you can track which aspects of your advertising are working and which are not – and so discover what is the most effective way to get noticed by potential customers.

Wendy Shand, a mother of two from Portsmouth, is another fledgling entrepreneur who has also used technology to her advantage. She decided to start up Tots to France (www.totstofrance.co.uk), an online company that offers safe, child-friendly holiday homes for families with babies and toddlers. She had the idea for her business after a fraught family holiday in France when her 18-month-old son fell into a swimming pool.

Again, instead of opening an expensive office Shand took a free online course in enterprise and spent £1,200 getting a website designed. She spent a total of £5,000 starting up the business. She says: 'Very little thought had been given to the needs of families travelling with small children and so I thought setting up an online business was a great way of addressing this niche in the market.'

Top tip

Make technology integral to your business rather than a last-minute add on. It will work better.

Profile: Richard Downs, founder of Iglu.com

As a child growing up in Wiltshire, Richard Downs' greatest passion was sport. The youngest of three children, he says: 'I liked being outdoors and playing football in the street. In fact sports kept me in touch with school.' So when he left school he went to study civil engineering at Loughborough University, primarily because of the university's renowned sporting facilities.

Downs went skiing for the first time at the age of 19 with the university's officer-training corps during a visit to Germany. 'I loved it from day one', he says.

On graduating Downs joined an accountancy firm and then worked for two investment banks. By the age of 29, however, he realised that he really wanted to do something of his own. So he enrolled on a two-year MBA course at the London Business School. He says: 'I did that with the specific intention of looking at business ideas and hopefully devoting part of my second year to setting up a company.'

His first idea was to start up an internet firm selling fat-free food imported from the United States. 'There was a low-fat revolution going on in New York and California and I could see what an opportunity the web could provide', he says. From the start he was convinced that success lay with embracing the technology that the internet was making possible.

As he researched the idea further, though, Downs realised that if the concept of fat-free food took off in Britain then the big super-markets would quickly muscle in on the market and start stocking it themselves. He says: 'One of the things I learnt at business school was how to differentiate ideas from opportunities. There are lots of ideas that are not opportunities. An opportunity needs to be sustainable and you need to be able to capture value and ideally differentiate it. In the process of that two-year MBA I probably looked at 50 ideas.'

Downs narrowed down his choices and decided to start up an online estate agency. But while on holiday with friends in California he changed his mind. 'I wanted to go skiing at Lake Tahoe but my friends wanted to drive down to San Diego', he says. 'I lost the vote and so moaned about it all the way. But we got talking and on the way my estate agency idea morphed into the idea of a ski agency.'

He wanted to create a firm that would sell ski holidays being offered by hundreds of different companies and provide up-to-date prices and availability. In return he would take a small percentage from each holiday sold. Downs says: 'At the time ski holidays were mainly sold using brochures from high-street travel agents. But there were a number of limitations to this. Travel agents would typically stock only three or four brochures, which would often be out-of-date because availability and prices change on a daily basis. People would go into a travel agent in the high street with friends and the travel agent would say "This holiday is not available, you need to choose again".'

He based his final-year MBA project on his idea of an online ski holiday provider and in 1998 launched his company with £25,000 raised through an overdraft and credit cards. He decided to call his company Iglu after some friends came up with the name at a dinner party. It seemed to be an ideal name for a company whose product was all about snow.

Then Downs got lucky. London Business School liked his idea so much that it invested £50,000 in return for a 15 per cent stake. Downs also managed to raise £75,000 from friends and family and got a small-business loan of £100,000, giving him a total of £250,000 to set up the company and the website.

He started by asking ski holiday firms if they wanted to advertise their holidays on the Iglu website. The response from both ski firms and customers was very positive and by late 1999, at the height of the dotcom boom, the company had attracted the interest of City institutions. Downs says: 'We had investment bankers crawling all over us wanting to float the company on the stock market.'

By the time he decided to take a closer look at the idea, however, the dotcom boom was over. He says: 'We thought we would wait until the ski season was over and that was when the door slammed shut. But actually it did us a big favour. I think if we had gone out there and raised gargantuan sums of money we would probably have frittered it away.'

But the sudden change in sentiment towards internet companies was hard to deal with. 'The door shut at a time when the business was not yet cash-flow positive and not profitable', says Downs, 'so we had 18 months during which we really had to turn the screws and focus on driving cash flow and profitability.'

The firm survived the turmoil, however, and in 2000 Downs started selling villa holidays via the Iglu website too. Iglu now also sells cruises and other specialist travel options such as Caribbean holidays and visits to Lapland. He says: 'I think there is a sense that those who survived that period must have something going for them.' Iglu.com is now set to have a turnover of £47 million in 2008 and employs around 150 people.

Downs, now 43 and married with two children, has a 30 per cent stake in the company shared with his management team. He says that the secret of his success has been to keep the online aspect of his business in perspective. 'We have fallen in love with the customer and not with technology. The dotcom graveyard is full of companies that fell in love with technology and forgot the customers', he says.

12

Think twice before parting with equity

When the late Dame Anita Roddick needed money to open her second Body Shop the bank refused to lend her any. So a friend, Ian McGlinn, agreed to give her the £4,000 she needed in return for a 50 per cent share of her business.

If Roddick had been able to get a bank loan for that £4,000 she would have simply been able to repay the money over time plus interest, which would have amounted to a few hundred pounds. Instead when she sold the Body Shop business in 2006 for £652 million, McGlinn, who by that time held 22.4 per cent of the business, received £146 million for his share.

The Body Shop experience perfectly illustrates the temptations and dangers of giving away equity in your business. At the time Dame Anita Roddick was giving away half of a business that amounted to a single shop, in other words half of not very much at all. And without the £4,000 from McGlinn, she would not have been able to open her second shop. There would be no Body Shop empire today and no business to sell for £652 million. On the other hand if she had managed to borrow the money from somewhere without giving away equity she would have been £146 million better off.

When you are starting out in business it can be extremely tempting to give away equity in return for an injection of cash or as payment in kind to people who are providing a service for you, for example to the designer who creates a website for you. With your fledgling business so small, parting with a share in it does not feel like you are giving away anything real that has any value. And even more enticing, unlike a bank loan or other borrowing, if the business fails then you do not have to pay your investor back a single penny.

As Keith Hunt, Managing Partner of business advisers Results International, puts it: 'The attractions of equity are that it is the least risky form of finance you can get. Unlike taking out a second mortgage on the house or spending your life savings it will never bankrupt you. It is all in the business – so if the business fails investors lose their money and you still get to keep your house.'

But the reality is that parting with equity in your fledgling business can work out far more expensive in the end than borrowing money or paying people with hard cash for their services. It is not just that the equity stake could one day be worth a fortune. It is that by parting with equity you get a shareholder who has a say in how you run your business. Someone who it is going to be very difficult to get rid of. If you decided to become an entrepreneur for the freedom and independence it promised, that could have far-reaching effects.

So how do you decide what to do? The first step is to look at whether there is any way of solving the problem without giving away equity, for example by borrowing the money you need from friends or family. If not, the next step is to decide how much you really need the money. Doug Richard, a former judge on the BBC television show *Dragons' Den* and Chairman of Library House, which provides research on private fast-growth companies, says you need to ask yourself whether the investment you would receive in return for selling equity would have a significant impact on the business.

'What sort of step-change does the investment permit? Are we talking about a huge acceleration of the business, or even more importantly a type of business where you need to be of a certain size before you are sustainable? If you are and you are not yet at that size, then I would say take the investment. At the end of the day it is much easier to make money by owning a smaller part of a fast growing and larger pie than it is to make money by owning the entire pie and having it worth nothing at all.'

Timing is crucial too. The difference in value between a business that is about to launch and one that launched six months ago and is now thriving is enormous – so hang on to your equity for as long as you can.

Richard says: 'Any entrepreneur who can get by without the cash for as long as possible is doing themselves a favour because whatever they can accomplish increases the value of the business and reduces the risk of the business. That means whatever equity they do sell, they can sell less for more.'

Of course there are some advantages in giving away equity to an investor at an early stage of your business. The investor may come with added benefits, such as experience of running a business, knowledge of the market you are entering and industry contacts. And having your website designer on board as an equity partner can be useful in the early years when the website is likely to need upgrading and improving.

Mike Alcock and Tony Reddington have taken a case by case approach towards giving away equity in their business, Atlantic Link, which makes e-learning software. Soon after starting up their business in 2002 they gave a 10 per cent share and a 5 per cent share of the equity to two directors they brought into the company. Alcock, the Managing Director, says: 'They were critical appointments and we wanted them as aligned as myself and Tony to the success of the business.'

A year later he and Reddington also gave a 20 per cent stake to the person who runs their software development arm, leaving the two founders with 32.5 per cent each. However, they decided against selling a further 20 per cent to investors in return for a £100,000 investment to market a new product because it did not feel right. Alcock says: 'Whilst the investment was key to the business, the people we were talking to wouldn't have been particularly key. They would have thrown some money at us but wouldn't have been involved on a day-to-day basis.' The business grew more slowly for a while but eventually orders came in and they managed without the investment.

It is vital to think through all the implications of having an equity partner on board because it is not a decision that is easily reversible. Steve Hinton, Chairman of QED Consulting, a business consultant says: 'For quite a few people the reason for having their own business is independence – but once you have got another shareholder then there is somebody else you need to report to and be accountable to. Think through your personal objectives and preferences and then those of the business and make sure they are congruent. If they are not you are going to have a hard time.'

He warns that it is very difficult to get rid of an equity partner, not least because you are unlikely to have access to the money you need to buy them out. He says: 'It is a bit like marriage. You shouldn't enter into it lightly.'

Top tip

The value of your equity will jump in a relatively short space of time as you move from being a start-up to running a self-sustaining business.

Profile: Justine Cather, founder of Burnt Sugar

Justine Cather learnt the hard way that it is never wise to make important life-changing decisions about your business when you are eight months pregnant with your first child. Panicking that she would not be able to run her fledgling traditional confectionary business as well as look after her baby, she gave away 50 per cent of her business to a local baker, Mark Campey. In return he set up a production facility to make the sweets and took on half the work of running the business.

She says: 'I was acting in a desperate way because I was wondering how I was going to cope. I thought if I didn't do this the business might fail.'

The partnership started off well Campey had an employee at the bakery who turned out to be great at making fudge. But it quickly became clear that Cather and her business partner had very different ideas about where Burnt Sugar should be heading. While Cather was determined to make Burnt Sugar a premium brand, Campey was more used to making non-premium bakery products. She says: 'We were just not on the same wavelength. It got to the stage where I was feeling really miserable about it.'

Luckily for Cather, after 18 months her husband Colin decided to leave his job in the corporate world and Campey agreed to sell his share in Burnt Sugar for £30,000 in cash. She says: 'It was a lot of money for us to come up with at the time but I felt so relieved because it was our business again. I could do what I liked and not have to battle with somebody who didn't see things the same way.'

Starting up her own business was not an automatic career path for Cather. Having spent much of her childhood abroad where her father worked for an oil company, she began to train as a teacher after leaving school. Then she went to Cyprus for a year with her husband Colin who was posted there with the army.

When Colin was posted back to Yorkshire Cather got a job managing an Oxfam charity shop. Then she joined Pizza Express, who sent her on a management course before giving her a restaurant to manage.

But in 1991, when she was 31, Cather realised she wanted to manage something of her own. Her mother had opened a small shop in Lyme Regis selling her home made fudge and sweets to holiday makers. It gave Cather an idea.

She says: 'I had visited her and seen how successful her business was and saw that people loved what she was doing. She just made sweets the only way she knew how, which was by hand and doing them properly. One of the things that really stood out was the way that she made the crumbly fudge which needed to be hand beaten to get the texture.'

She decided that the demand for proper homemade fudge might extend beyond holiday makers in Lyme Regis. She says: 'Tourists were saying they wished they could buy it when they were at home too, rather than just once a year when they were on holiday. I just thought there was a gap in the market there – we have a lovely heritage of traditional sweets in this country but they have been really neglected over the years. Nobody was really giving sweets the care and attention that they gave chocolate.'

With her mother's blessing Cather got to work. She found a design company near where she lived in Hull to design some high quality packaging and took a stand at a trade fair. The packaging was expensive but it got her sweets noticed. She says: 'The gift boxes cost a fortune and people told me I couldn't spend that much on packaging. But I went for it and I am glad I did because it got me instantly noticed.'

Her mother agreed to supply her with all the sweets she needed for the first year until Cather could set up her own production facility. She says: 'That really did help me because it allowed me to test the water.'

She started selling boxes of sweets directly to upmarket delicatessens. Her husband had by now left the army to work for Unilever and volunteered to take a stall selling the sweets one weekend a month at Borough Market in London. It was a great way of gauging customer reaction and also brought in around £300, which helped cash flow.

It was at that point Cather became pregnant and brought in the local baker as a business partner with a 50 per cent share in the business.

Having bought back the stake, Cather and her husband ran the business from offices above the production facility for a year. Then they started making some big changes to the way the business was run. First they took on a Non-executive Director, John Kennedy, who had been Operations Director at Green and Blacks, the organic chocolate company. Through him they also found a Sales Director, Doug Struthers, who came on board as a partner taking a one-third share in the business. Then they found a local company to take over the manufacture of the sweets, with the original fudge maker still in charge.

Burnt Sugar is now expected to have a turnover of £3 million in 2008 and is stocked by Harvey Nichols and supermarkets including Waitrose, Sainsbury's and Tesco.

Now 40 and married with two children, Cather thinks the secret of her success has been not giving up. She says: 'When I was pregnant I was thinking "This is really hard, why am I doing this?" But when it all works there isn't a better feeling.'

Not surprisingly her advice to others is to be wary of rushing into a partnership and parting with equity without really thinking it through first. 'Make sure you are in a partnership with someone who has the same vision. That is where I slipped up. I thought production was my main objective and I didn't think about the bigger picture.'

13

Don't assume your customers will find you

It would be lovely to think that you could simply launch a fantastic product or service onto the market and sit back as everyone immediately rushed out to buy it. Unfortunately in this hugely complex, multi-layered, product-packed world that we live in, no matter how good your product or service is, you cannot simply hope that customers are going to find you. You must find them – as quickly and as cheaply as possible. The process is called marketing and no matter how much the word terrifies you, you have got to do it.

The secret is to tell prospective customers about your product in a way that grabs their attention. Remember all those television adverts for car insurance with the annoying jingles that you cannot get out of your head? Well the makers of the advert know that jingle is annoying too – and they also know that the next time you have to renew your car insurance you are likely to be so overwhelmed by the number of insurers in the market that you will remember the name of their company and call them for a quote.

But clever marketing is not just for big companies. Fledgling entrepreneurs can use smart tactics too. When Rick Stainton decided to start Smyle, his events company, he wanted to make sure it got noticed by the right people. So he drew up a list of the 500 richest people in the country and sent each a personal letter with a £20 note attached, thanking them for the 30 seconds it would take to read the letter. 'I knew I needed to get the letter past the personal assistants who screen all the mail,' he says 'and that once my letter got in front of the right person I would need to get their attention in a matter of seconds.'

It was a brave tactic. At a cost of £10,000, the marketing ploy ate up all the money Stainton had to start up Smyle. It also cost him time. Before posting the letters, printed on top-quality paper and with handwritten envelopes, he had spent nine months researching his potential clients.

Fortunately the idea worked. About 70 per cent of the people he wrote to responded, and more than half of them returned the £20 to donate to Inspire, the spinal injuries charity that Stainton has supported since breaking his neck 10 years ago. Thanks to his innovative mailshot, Smyle was asked to organise three events, giving him £250,000 of business. As a result the company had a turnover of £1 million in its first year.

Stainton says about his opening gambit: 'It was a huge risk. If it hadn't worked we would have been in trouble. But if you really want to make a big splash it doesn't have to cost a lot of money, it just has to be something that will really tickle the right audience.'

Graham Green, founder of Meerkat communications agency and now a marketing consultant, says: 'Marketing is not about spending lots of money. It is about thinking and creativity and even the smallest business can do that. When Rutherford was splitting the atom, he said: "We have no money therefore we shall have to think". For small businesses it comes down to the same thing.'

Green says that even for the tiniest firm marketing should not be seen as an optional extra: 'Marketing is not only something that small businesses can do, it is something they have to do. There is absolutely no point in having the best product in the world unless you go out and sell it to people.'

While some marketing tactics will be more effective than others, the secret is to keep trying. The one thing that definitely does not work is sitting round talking about it – because then you never actually do anything.

The online law firm Lawyers Direct decided to draw attention to the fact that it can provide top-quality lawyers at a fraction of the usual cost because of its lower overheads. It did this by including in the goody bags at a Department of Trade and Industry awards ceremony 1,000 bags of peanuts with the Lawyers Direct logo and the slogan: 'These days you have to be nuts to pay for overhead.' At a cost of £1 a bag, the exercise cost them just £1,000.

James Knight, Managing Director of Lawyers Direct, says: 'For us it is all about saving overheads, so it was important to get that message across in a very clear, memorable way.' The ploy worked well. In the weeks after the ceremony, Lawyers Direct gained seven new clients who had been at the event and liked the firm's unconventional approach.

Indeed, small businesses that have managed to carve out a niche may not need to spend any money at all on marketing their product. Gü Puds, for example, which makes gooey chocolate puddings, recently carried on its packaging a tear-off cardboard strip that offered customers a free Johnny Depp DVD. At first glance it looked like an expensive marketing idea, but the cost of the strip and the DVDs was borne by Screen Select, an internet DVD business that wanted to boost its profile. Gu Puds paid nothing.

The two companies were brought together by Packaging Media, a company that has patented the tear-off strip, called More Inside. Keran Turakhia, Managing Director of Packaging Media, says: 'Traditionally, if Gu Puds wanted to offer its customers a free Johnny Depp DVD it would have had to pay for it itself and it would hope that by increasing the sales of its chocolate puddings it would recover that cost. But this technology means that a small business like Gu Puds can do things that would traditionally be only for big companies – and it doesn't cost anything.'

Turakhia has set up a similar arrangement for another small business, cake maker Fabulous Bakin' Boys, which will offer its customers half-price holidays under a tear-off strip. He says that small firms in particular have the potential to make the most of ingenious marketing. 'The reason they can do this even though they are small businesses is because they have a niche market. They may think they cannot afford to do an on-pack promotion but they have more value than they think.'

Top tip

Creative thinking can go a long way to make up for a lack of cash.

Profile: James Murray Wells, founder of Glasses Direct

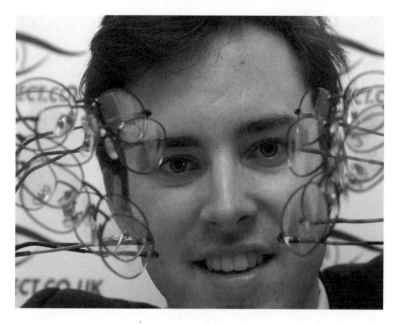

James Murray Wells had not planned to become one of the UK's youngest successful entrepreneurs. Born and brought up in Gloucestershire and sent to boarding school at the age of nine, he dreamt of getting a job in the theatre as a director or manager.

But while at university studying English he decided he ought to pursue a less risky profession such as law. The problem was that deep down he knew it was not what he really wanted. 'I was racking my brains for a business idea or an opportunity that would save me from law school,' says Murray Wells. The answer came to him when he had to buy a new pair of glasses. 'They cost £150 and I thought that was way too much. What the hell was I paying for? They were just a bit of plastic and a bit of glass', he says. 'It didn't make sense.'

He started researching the market while he was supposed to be revising for his finals, looking up market reports in the university library and trying to track down manufacturers via the internet. He eventually found a laboratory in Lancashire that agreed to make a pair of glasses from the prescription he sent in. One week later they arrived – with a bill for £5. 'That was the wholesale cost. It shocked me because I had just paid £150 for the same thing', he says.

So Murray Wells borrowed £1,000 from his student loan and, working from the front room of his parents' house, hired a student web developer at £6 an hour to help him design a website where customers could enter their prescriptions and order spectacles. The website went live in July 2004 with all prescription glasses priced at £15.

Realising that he needed to seek out his customers rather than expecting them to find him, Murray Wells started publicising his service by handing out flyers in the street. He also quickly dreamt up other ways of publicising his business. He says: 'I used to jump on trains at Bristol Temple Meads and put flyers on the tables and then get off the train before it left the station. So people had two hours to sit there and read about Glasses Direct.'

Within days Murray Wells was receiving so many calls he had to get friends to answer the phone. 'At one point I had eight friends working from my home and my mum was the staff canteen in the kitchen', he says. 'We were laying cables into my parents' spare bedroom.' By September he had to employ a call centre and had moved into an office. He says: 'It was a real rollercoaster. The first few months it was really full on.'

As his success grew, however, Murray Wells began to face strong opposition from high-street opticians who were angry at his low prices. He says the opticians put so much pressure on his supplier that the firm refused to continue making spectacles for him. With no glasses to sell, Murray Wells was forced to close his website for a few weeks until he was able to find another supplier in Gloucestershire.

Despite the setback he says he enjoyed the challenge. 'I loved it. At school I was always getting into trouble – things like being chased round the golf course at night for smoking – and it gave me a bit of a kick.'

With the business up and running again he was able to raise £100,000 from friends and family, half of which came from his father, an investment analyst. He says: 'My dad wouldn't give me any money to start with because he said I had to prove the business would work. However once I had proven the model quite a lot of people were willing to invest.'

The following year, in 2005, Murray Wells held another round of fundraising, this time to raise £500,000. Then in 2007 he raised yet more investment with the injection of £3 million by venture capitalists into the business. He says: 'Everyone wanted to invest so I was able to go out and pick the right guys.'

A pair of glasses bought via the website costs from £15 and customers can opt for lenses of different tints and thicknesses. Although at present customers still need to have an eye test at an optician's before they are able to buy their glasses online using their prescription, Murray Wells eventually hopes to have a team of mobile opticians visiting customers at home. Customers requiring varifocal lenses already receive a visit from an optician to take the measurements needed. He hopes to make Glasses Direct a household name in the UK and plans eventually to expand the brand overseas. Glasses Direct now employs 35 people and is expected to have sales of £10 million in 2008.

Still only 25 and now with a stake of around 30 per cent in the company, Murray Wells admits he is primarily motivated by the desire to make money. He says: 'Financial reward is a really big thing. I am doing this to make money for myself and my shareholders and if we can be rewarded for the kind of risks we have taken, then that's great.'

He thinks the secret of his success is being open to new opportunities, an attitude he learnt from his parents. 'Being an entrepreneur is about having your mind open to when a problem arises and then seizing the opportunity and going for it', he says. 'It's a question of whether you get up off the sofa and put down the Playstation, or whether you just sit there.'

He has this advice for other budding entrepreneurs: 'Start small and grow big. A lot of people want big offices as soon as they start, but we started really small and so the risks were minimal and I was able to test the business first and find out whether it worked.'

14

Think big

If you spotted Smart Beauty's hair colouring products next to those of its competitors Wella and L'Oreal on the shelves of a supermarket, you might assume you were looking at the products of a company that was of a similar size. The packaging is every bit as professional as its rivals and the products are stocked everywhere from Asda to Sainsbury's and Tesco. If you then checked out Smart Beauty's slick website, www.smartbeauty.eu, you would still come away with the same impression, perhaps assuming that having an eu suffix to the website address indicated a company with European-wide operations.

In reality Smart Beauty employs just two people in addition to its two founder directors and this year will have a turnover of only £1.5 million – a tiny fraction of the annual turnover chalked up by its competitors. But as Smart Beauty's directors have realised, just because you are a small business it does not have to mean that you look or act like a small business, particularly when you are operating in an industry where bigger is regarded as better. Madeleine Mansfield, who set up the company with co-founder Michael Rusby in 2002, says they have deliberately tried to look big and think big in a market dominated by giants.

The first step was the website. She says: 'Having the website address www.smartbeauty.eu means that we could be absolutely anywhere. It doesn't pigeonhole us in any way because it is not a specific country or region.'

In an effort to punch above their weight the two of them also take a very large stand every year at the Clothes Show exhibition to show that they are a serious player in the market. Mansfield says: 'It definitely gives that impression that we are a bigger company and are here to stay.'

Their third ploy has been to get featured as much as possible in the hair and beauty magazines whose readers are their target market – for free, by giving away Smart Beauty products in competitions. She says: 'We wanted to get our name out there as quickly as possible but we can't afford to spend thousands on advertising. This means that we gain page space without having to pay for it.'

One of the biggest drawbacks to starting up your own business is that you are likely to start out as a small business. And the biggest disadvantage of being small, as any child will tell you, is that it can be hard to make your voice heard amid the clamour of the bigger children in the playground. The good news is that no matter how small you are with a little bit of effort and imagination you can punch above your weight and get your message across.

Initially it could be something as simple as printing your catalogue on high quality paper. Or making sure that the office phone is answered in a professional manner, or devising a logo for the business. Or even giving your staff matching uniforms to wear.

John Thompson, National Business Advisory Partner at Baker Tilly, an accountancy firm, says that thinking big is not only useful for establishing yourself in the market – it is essential if you want your business to grow. He says: 'One of the best ways to think about it is to consider how you would like your company to be in five years' time – and act like that now. If you have a turnover of £3 million now but you plan to reach £20 million then imagine what the look and feel of your business will be then, the structures you might have in place, the messages you will be giving to the market and so on – and begin to act like that now. Acting big is like future-proofing the business.'

The first step, he says, is to build an external team of advisers, such as lawyers and accountants, who will be appropriate not for where your business is at present but where you intend it to be in a few years' time. 'The temptation is to hire the cheapest advisers you can get. But when you start entering into negotiations with larger organisations one of the first things they are going to look at is who your advisers are. If your advisers are Bloggs and Bloggs from round the corner and nobody has heard of them then rightly or wrongly the immediate impression will be, well, who are these guys? Whereas if you have chosen a firm with a reasonable amount of clout and expertise, that a person might look at your advisers' website and say, oh that is not a bad firm. These guys are serious players because they have serious advisers.'

The next step is to build an internal team that reflects where you want the business to be. And that might mean hiring a professional finance director ahead of when you actually need one. Thompson says: 'If you need somebody in a year's time, why don't you need them now? You should be trying to get ahead of the game all the time. Having a professional team in place internally as well as externally is a strong message to the market.'

Thinking big and acting accordingly has other benefits too. First, it signals to your potential customers and suppliers that you are here to stay – and that as you grow they will be able to grow too. Customers want to be assured that a business they are dealing with is likely to still be in existence this time next year. So if your business looks like it is going places you are more likely to win their custom.

Mark Riminton, Director of Shirlaws, a business-coaching company, says small firms need to think hard about how their business looks to an outsider, especially when they are trying to break into a new market. If the first impression of their business does not meet the customers' expectations then they are never going to get anywhere.

He says: 'You must decide how you need to look in order to enter the market you are going for. If I am a one-man band is it realistic for me to expect to win a project from the Fire Brigade or the Department of Social Services? Probably not.'

Second, thinking big signals to your staff that they are with a dynamic company that is really going places. This not only makes them feel good about being part of your team and more motivated to invest time and energy into making your company great, it also reassures them that they made the right decision taking a job with you in the first place. Which means that they are more likely to want to stay, and that others are more likely to want to join.

Top tip

Size matters – but having the right attitude matters more.

Profile: Hilary Devey, founder of Pall-Ex

When Hilary Devey was growing up in Bolton she dreamt of going to university and becoming a lawyer. But her father, who ran a central-heating company, became ill and so at the age of 17 she had to go out to work to help support the family.

Her first job was with a haulage company. Then she spent the next few years doing a variety of jobs including selling insurance door to door. Next she joined a large logistics business and at the age of 31 became the national sales manager for TNT, the parcel-delivery company.

But at the age of 38 Devey decided it was time to do something for herself. It was not exactly ideal timing. She was earning a good salary and was a single mother with a seven-year-old son. 'I wanted to be more in control of my own destiny and I had a burning ambition to achieve something', she says. 'It was a big risk because I was earning a comfortable salary, but I thought it was now or never.'

She also hoped that working for herself would give her more time to spend with her son.

She initially set up a consultancy advising firms on sales and marketing. But one day while helping a company to set up a haulage scheme Devey found herself in an office in Wales listening to the owner talking to a customer on the phone.

She says: 'I heard him say that they could do a delivery to Scotland but it would not get there until the following Wednesday. For me, coming from a parcels background, that was like going back 20 to 30 years. I asked the haulier why he couldn't deliver until the next Wednesday and he said it would not be cost-effective until they could fill a whole vehicle.' It was an epiphany for Devey. She says: 'I thought "There has to be an easier way than this".'

Right from the start she had a big goal in her mind. She decided to create a central hub so that hauliers from different parts of the UK could bring deliveries on pallets from their own area and swap them for deliveries going back there. That way each haulier would simply have to drive between their region and the hub rather than to multiple destinations, thereby increasing efficiency and reducing costs.

To keep the start-up costs down she decided to set up the hub as a network of members, with hauliers paying an annual fee to join. It was a bold plan. At the beginning of 1996 she raised £112,000 by selling her house and car. Then she set about recruiting hauliers to her network, studying demographics and then travelling hundreds of miles a week to see them and sell the concept. She says: 'I set myself certain criteria – the members had to be financially solvent and they had to have certain operational standards.'

In such a male-dominated industry she got a mixed response. 'I think some thought: "Who is this madwoman, what is she talking about?".' Gradually, though, hauliers started to realise that her business model made sense. 'My system gave them the luxury of telling their customers that they could deliver their pallets the next day', she says. 'I sold the concept to them on the idea of "every postcode, every day".'

By the end of the year she had signed up 29 hauliers and was ready to launch the business. She had worked out that logistically the hub needed to be somewhere in the Midlands. As she could not afford to build a facility of her own, she rented a disused Second World War aircraft hangar in Leicestershire. 'It had no running water, no electricity and chemical loos', she says.

Right from the start Devey was strict about how the hub would be run. 'I wrote operational procedures and made members abide by them. If they didn't, I expelled them from the network. After I had done that once, they knew I meant business and that I would not compromise my standards. The ethos of the company is that they treat each other's freight as they would treat their own. It's really strictly enforced.'

Remarkably, for the first three years the business performed exactly as Devey had forecast in her business plan. The first year it made a loss, the second year it broke even and the third year it was in profit.

The plan to spend more time with her son did not work out quite so well, however. She was soon working 20-hour days, seven days a week. So she bought him a go-kart and let him drive round the hub while she worked.

She says: 'Failure was not an option. It just wasn't in my vocabulary. I knew I was going to succeed. If you don't have faith in yourself, then nobody else will have faith in you.' By 2002 the business had grown so much that Devey was able to buy some land and build a hub from scratch complete with canteen facilities for the drivers.

Pall-Ex, which Devey still wholly owns, now has more than 100 members and regularly deals with 10,000 pallets a night at the hub. The company employs 250 people at the site and will have a turnover of nearly £21 million in 2008. Still thinking big, Devey now hopes to roll out the concept across Europe.

Now aged 51 and remarried, Devey thinks the secret of her success in such a male-dominated industry has simply been to be herself. She says: 'I'm very straight-talking and I think hauliers respond to that. They may not like me, but hopefully I've earned their respect now.'

She has some advice for women seeking to emulate her success: 'Don't be put off by working in a man's world. Yes it's hard and yes you have something to prove but there isn't a glass ceiling. You can go as far and as fast as you want to go. You just have to be tenacious and focused and very disciplined.'

15

Make it easy for luck to strike

Most successful entrepreneurs seem to have an element of luck playing a part in their success. Either they happened to be in the right place at the right time, or they happened to meet someone at the right moment who wanted to invest in their venture. Perhaps a prime location shop became empty just as they needed to rent it. Or demand in their particular market they were entering just happened to take off weeks before their product was launched.

The truth is there is a lot more to these moments of luck than is apparent at first glance. Yes these entrepreneurs have been lucky, but usually only because they have first spent much time and energy creating the framework in which luck can flourish. They found the investor not because they happened to start talking about their idea to that one person, but because they talked about their idea to everyone they met. They found the perfect shop to rent not because they just happened to notice it but because they had been looking at every single building to rent within a 20 mile radius and had built relationships with the estate agents and property owners who operated in that market.

The good news is that it is possible for you too to have your share of luck. You just have to be ready and prepared for every opportunity that comes your way. And then do your very best to increase the number of opportunities that come your way by going out to look for them.

Opportunities can come in all shapes and sizes. An opportunity can arise when you are chatting to someone at a party. It can arise when you are visiting a new place. It can even arise when you are sitting on a train or going to the theatre. Or breaking your leg and ending up in hospital. All you have to do is make sure you are prepared for it when it comes along.

Say you have landed the opportunity to meet a potential major customer for your product. Before you even enter the meeting room you should have decided exactly what you want to get out of the deal. Not just in terms of price, but in terms of other factors, such as supply terms and length of contract. You should also have thought hard about what the other side is likely to be looking for so you have a good idea in advance where areas of agreement and contention are likely to arise.

Mike Bird, a partner with Kepner-Tregoe, a management consultancy and training company, says: 'Most negotiations are won or lost before you go into the room. Before you go in you need to work out what your "musts" are and what your "wants" are. In other words, what's absolutely critical – what you have to have or else the deal is dead – and what things you'd like to have and want to maximise. You must be very clear in advance which is which. Before you go in, you also need to work out what your opposite number's "musts" and "wants" are. If your "musts" are incompatible there is no point in even having a meeting.'

Cristina Stuart, founder of the Speak First business training company, says: 'If you know what the other side wants, you can anticipate what their reactions might be and plan your moves in advance so that you're not surprised.'

Doug Richard, a former judge of BBC television's *Dragons' Den* and the Chairman of Library House, which researches fast-growing private companies, agrees that the secret to finding luck is to be completely ready for it when it appears. He says: 'Luck frequently comes in the form of the thing you did not expect and therefore the only way you can prepare for luck is not to be blind to opportunity when it presents itself. Be open to everything around you, don't shutter yourself. There is nothing wrong with an element of opportunism in your soul when you are an entrepreneur, because luck is not going to happen in the way you expect it to.'

Kim Fletcher, business adviser at Business Link in Kent, says that there is one simple way to increase the opportunities that present themselves to you – and that is to network with other people wherever and whenever you can. He says: 'If you sit at home and don't talk to anybody then nothing is going to happen. But if you are really aware of what is going on around you and who is doing what, that is when you spot opportunities. And the bigger and wider your network and the more people you talk to, the more opportunities you see and the more chances you get. That is because people are aware of what you are doing and therefore how your service or product fits with them.'

It all comes down to hard work. 'What people call luck is really them getting a return on all of that intangible work that they have put in. The people who think: "Oh he is a lucky devil" don't realise just how well connected that person is. Luck is about ensuring that even the smallest stone does not go unturned.'

Sarah Rogers seized an unlikely opportunity that directly led to her starting up her own business, a handmade jewellery business called Dragon and Phoenix. The mother of three young children under six, she decided to visit her brother in Hong Kong for a short break on her own. While she was there she visited China where she came across semi-precious stones that she thought would be perfect to make into necklaces and bracelets.

Her sister-in-law introduced her to someone who could turn her beads into necklaces and Rogers brought back 15 completed pieces, which she immediately sold to friends. She realised she might have stumbled upon a business idea and so asked her sister-in-law to send her more stones. The business took off and has thrived.

Rogers now has a studio of her own where she designs and makes bespoke jewellery. She says: 'I think luck is out there all the time. It is really about grabbing the opportunities that luck puts in your way and being receptive to them.'

Ultimately your ability to seize opportunities boils down to your ability to spot them in the first place. And the best way to do that is to assume that every single situation or event you encounter contains within it the seed of an opportunity for you. All you have to do is find it.

David Lewis is a neuropsychologist who runs The MindLab, a collective of academics that advises businesses. He says: 'If you meet a man on the train and tell him your idea and he turns out to be a multimillionaire who gives you the money for a start-up, that is lucky – but if you had not already prepared your business idea and seized the moment to persuade this guy it would have passed by. Luck is about recognising the opportunities as they arise.'

Top tip

Memorise your business plan. There is nothing more off-putting than someone who does not know their business inside out.

Profile: James Hibbert, founder of Dress2Kill

James Hibbert got the idea of making bespoke suits when a tailor came to his office to measure him up for one. 'He had really bad breath and no personality. But as I was getting measured up some colleagues popped in and he ended up selling about 20 suits that day', says Hibbert. 'I went back to my desk and I just couldn't get it out of my head. I thought there had to be a niche there.'

Hibbert was brought up in East Horsley, Surrey, where his father became the first person to sell flat-pack furniture by mail order in the UK. Perhaps because of this insight into being an entrepreneur, Hibbert himself got into the idea of making money from a young age. At the age of seven he grew cacti and sold them on a tray outside his house to passing commuters.

He did not excel at school, however, and after dropping out of sixth form halfway through his A levels got a job with a company selling fax machines and photocopiers. Hibbert discovered he loved selling and after six months, aged 18, he left to start up a business selling fax machines and photocopiers with a friend. They began with a single fax machine which they leased out. They ran the business from Hibbert's parents' home before opening a shop in East Horsley.

The business did well, providing Hibbert with enough money to put down a deposit on a house. But after two years the pair decided they wanted to get some corporate experience and closed it down. Hibbert joined an overnight courier firm and stayed there eight years before getting a job with a recruitment consultant.

It was while working there that he got the idea for the suit business. His girlfriend's father encouraged him and put him in touch with Shirley Biggs, a retired lady with a retail background. Fired up by her enthusiasm, Hibbert decided to take the plunge and set up Itsuits, a bespoke tailoring service, with Biggs as a business partner. They put in £5,000 each and went to see a manufacturer who taught them how to measure somebody for a suit. Then, to get the business off the ground, they called up 15 friends each and offered to make them a bespoke suit in the hope that if they liked them they would recommend the service to other people.

It was a disaster. 'Ten of the suits didn't fit at all', says Hibbert. 'Our friends were saying "What on earth are you doing?". We had to do a lot of remakes.'

They got the suits right eventually but the first year was a real slog, culminating in sales of £87,500. The second year was even harder and sales actually fell, to £72,000.

'It was pretty demotivating', says Hibbert. Having saved only three months' salary from his previous job to live on while the business got going he was soon struggling and was forced to remortgage his house twice.

By the end of the second year the business was close to insolvency and Hibbert realised he had to act. He decided to change the name of the company to Dress2Kill and start again with a fresh approach. He also decided it was time to give luck the opportunity to strike.

Desperate for advice on how to turn the company round, he wrote a letter to Virgin boss Sir Richard Branson and another one to Charles Dunstone, the founder of Carphone Warehouse, asking them if he could have an hour of their time in return for making them a suit. Incredibly, both agreed and within a week Hibbert had met both.

'I didn't know them at all but I went to see them and they were both brilliant', he says. Branson offered to let Hibbert promote his bespoke service in the Virgin Upper Class airport lounge and put him in touch with Virgin Brides, where Hibbert offered his suit-making services to grooms. Inspired by the advice he received, Hibbert improved Dress2Kill's website and started promoting the business with the help of a public-relations agency.

He also took a short course at Cranfield Business School, which proved to be a turning point for the company. While he was there Hibbert realised that the key to growing the business was the place where it was conducted. Most of his customers preferred to come to Dress2Kill's offices for their suit fitting rather than be visited at their work.

'Suddenly it dawned on me', he says. 'I asked them, why are you coming in here? And they said it was because they wanted to know who they were buying from. If we went out with a load of swatches and a bag, they wouldn't know who Dress2Kill was.'

Hibbert liked it that customers were coming to visit him rather than the other way round, but the office was small and tatty. So in 2006 he revamped the company, spending £100,000 fitting out a shop where customers could come and be measured for a suit in nice surroundings while having a glass of champagne. To complete the experience, Hibbert opened a male grooming parlour on the first floor where customers could have a shave and a haircut.

Dress2Kill also opened its own workshop to make most of its suits, which range in price from £350 to £825, and recently opened its third outlet. The business is expected to have a turnover of £5 million in 2008.

Hibbert admits to making one mistake. When he started up the company he gave his brother and a friend a 10 per cent share each in the company in return for an investment of £1,000. Fortunately for him, two years later they both agreed to sell the shares back for £1,300.

Now 36 and married, he says the secret of his success was to change direction when he did. His other secret had been finding a business partner who shared his vision. 'That is absolutely key,' says Hibbert, 'because there are times when you are down and you need lifting up. Shirley Biggs has been a rock to me.'

16

Learn how to sell

At some point while starting up your business you are likely to find yourself in a meeting room trying to persuade someone from another business to buy your product or service. For many budding entrepreneurs this can be a nerve-wracking experience, and with good reason. If the person on the other side of the table is from a large organisation with substantial buying power then their decision could have an enormous impact on your business. It could even affect whether it gets off the ground in the first place.

The good news is that there are several things you can do to improve your selling skills. The key is to do all your preparation before you get into the meeting, instead of trying to wing it on the spot once you are inside.

The first step is to make sure you know your product or service inside out. Identify the things that make it stand out from its competitors and decide where it fits into the market. Stuart Fisher, Principal Consultant with Boxwood Group, a business performance improvement company, says: 'Pinpoint the things that make it unique. Understand where your opportunity is in the marketplace and what your aspirations are for your product. You also need to understand what your competitors are doing and find out what the threats are to your product.'

Next make sure you are charging a proper price for your product. Many first time entrepreneurs tend to under-charge for their goods because they lack confidence and so undervalue the cost of their own time spent on the busi-ness. But selling things too cheaply is counterproductive because customers think they are getting an inferior product or service and so will be put off.

To avoid doing this you need to look at what your competitors are charging and then analyse where your product or service fits into the market. If you find this hard to do then ask someone to help you, such as your account-ant or another business owner. Being in business is all about projecting confidence and if you are meek about your busi-ness then it will not be around for very long.

That also means knowing your production costs inside out. One mistake many small food producers make when approaching large supermarket chains about supplying them with their products, for example, is they enter into negotiations without fully understanding what their costs of production are. In other words not just the price of the ingredients but also how much it costs to package, trans-port and distribute their products. Without a clear set of figures or a real understanding of how they are going to make money out of an agreement, the small producers can end up accepting a deal based on prices and quantities that leave them feeling financially squeezed and struggling to make any money out of the arrangement.

The next step is to think carefully about what the buyer is actually looking for. Try to work out what their motivation is for buying your product. You can do this by finding out as much as you can about their company – by checking out their website, reading their annual report, and by using the internet to look at any references to them, for example in the trade press. Are they looking for a product to help them solve a problem? Or are they trying to expand into a new area and your product would help them do it? Look at their current list of products and find out if there is a gap that your product would fill.

Many big supermarket chains, for example, are now actively looking for regional products that strongly reflect the locality in which they are produced. And for that reason they are happy for a producer to supply just a handful of stores in their local area, something that is ideal for small producers.

Lynda Whitcombe started supplying her Plantation Cottage jellies to supermarket chain Waitrose in 2007 after the regional food body Heart of England Fine Foods suggested she show it some samples. She now supplies five local Waitrose stores. Whitcombe, who is based in Bricklehampton in Worcestershire, turned an outbuilding into a dedicated kitchen to make her jellies, which are produced using home-grown herbs from her garden.

She says: 'I had been selling my jellies in the local farmers' market and I thought I was never going to be able to make enough for Waitrose. But it is like supplying the local deli. Initially the process was a bit daunting but once I got to know the local Waitrose buyer she was very reassuring.'

Once you are actually in a meeting with a buyer, never criticise your competitors. This is not just good etiquette, it is good business sense. Fisher says: 'It is always detrimental to your organisation if you exploit a competitor's weaknesses or misfortunes for your own advancement. If you play to the strengths of your own product it puts you in much better standing. Keep to the facts you have for your product or services.'

Make sure too that the conversation is a two-way process. If you launch into a 10-minute monologue about what the benefits of your product are to a buyer you will never find out what they are actually looking for. Listen as well as talk.

Seemingly trivial things matter too. Martin King is Business Development Director of the Read Group which creates databases for direct mail companies. He always advises his salespeople to stand rather than sit in the waiting area before they are called into a meeting. 'If a salesman is sitting down and drinking coffee, he looks clumsy. If he is standing up, he seems eager and ready to go and it looks better', he says. 'Immediately he is at the same visual level and can shake hands.'

Once in the meeting, King advises people to go easy on the coffee and sandwiches if they are offered them. 'People inevitably spill coffee. And there is nothing worse than loading your plate with sandwiches and then shoving them down your throat. You are not there to eat. It is hard enough to get into that meeting and to get someone interested in buying your product, so why jeopardise it?'

Finally, do not take any of it personally. Sales negotiations are about doing business and emotions are best left at the door. In particular do not start acting like a downtrodden underdog just because your business is the smaller and less experienced business of the two. Large organisations such as supermarkets have a duty to their shareholders to get the best deal they can out of their suppliers and tough negotiating is simply part of that. Whatever you might think, they are not picking on you just because your business is small. If they are playing hard ball in the negotiations then do not feel aggrieved and do not feel resentful. Simply play hard ball right back at them. Remember that you can always walk away.

Top tip

Never promise anything you cannot deliver.

Profile: Robyn Jones, founder of Charlton House

As a child Robyn Jones loved cooking. Her mother also loved her daughter to cook – but not for the same reasons. Jones says: 'I thought mum loved the food I cooked for her. But I realised later on that it wasn't actually the food she loved, it was the fact that I cleaned up the kitchen so well afterwards that it was cleaner and tidier than when I started.'

Born in Sutton Coldfield in the West Midlands, Jones was the youngest of three girls. Her mother was a teacher and her father was an engineer but when he was made redundant he got a job in a tramway museum.

Jones herself was never particularly academic and left school at 16. She says: 'I didn't want to do my A levels because I thought it would involve a lot of reading. I didn't like reading because when I was young my great-aunt used to come and stay with us and during the summer holidays I would have to sit and read to her. I would end up with my eyes watering from reading and I would see all my friends outside playing while I was sitting there. I hated it and it completely put me off.'

Instead she took a diploma in hotel management and then joined a management trainee course in Cambridge, working for different organizations. She says: 'I went from chief bottle washer to assistant chef to senior area manager. I just worked my way up with various catering firms.'

She also briefly joined the Potato Marketing Board as an adviser and at the age of 29 she joined Higgs and Hill, a construction firm, where she ran the building site canteens. Unfortunately after two years recession hit. The whole catering division was closed down and in 1991 Jones was made redundant. It was a horrible shock. 'I never for one moment thought I'd be without a job because I had always been very structured and always planned my next job and what I was going to do. I had my career planned out in my head.'

She went for a few job interviews but her heart was not in it. So Jones decided to take the plunge and start up her own contract catering company. With the support of her husband and an enterprise allowance from the government of £50 a week, she converted the spare room into an office. Then she started cold-calling prospective clients to see if they wanted her to run their staff restaurant.

Starting up a business from scratch, however, proved to be a lot harder than she had envisaged. With no catering contracts already in operation for prospective clients to see Jones found it hard to persuade people to take her on. She says: 'Prospective clients didn't want to take the risk of being my first client. It was very hard at the beginning. It is such a competitive business that just trying to get someone to talk to me was a challenge.'

She realised she had to learn how to sell her services in the most effective way possible. 'I am a very target-driven person so I would say to myself I couldn't have a coffee until I had spoken to a prospective client and got an appointment. And then I couldn't have any lunch until I had got another one.'

In the end it took several months to get her first contract, running the staff restaurants for the charity Guide Dogs for the Blind. Even then it was difficult to get other contracts because the staff restaurants were in Reading and potential London clients were reluctant to travel out to see them.

Jones also made a big mistake. 'I put all my energy and hard work into starting up the contract for Guide Dogs for the Blind and making sure that it was successful', she says, 'and I stopped putting any effort into getting new clients. Then six months on when the Guide Dogs contract was bedded in, I phoned the potential clients back. But they said because I hadn't phoned back earlier they thought I wasn't interested and so they had given the contract to someone else. So I missed a few good opportunities because I hadn't juggled.'

Eventually she won a contract to run the staff restaurant at Bupa, the private health insurer. Then Sony UK's head office asked her to run their staff restaurant too.

It was a big turning point. As a result Jones hired an area manager and moved the business out of her home and into a serviced office. She also started positioning the business where she wanted it to be. 'At the time our competitors were telling prospective clients what it was they wanted', she says. 'But we asked our clients what they would like. We would tailor-make our service to them so it was not an off-the-shelf ready-made box.'

The strategy worked. Charlton House is now expected to have a turnover of £76 million in 2008 and employs nearly 2,000 people. The firm's clients include the American Embassy and the Civil Aviation Authority.

Now aged 47 and married with two children, Jones still owns 95 per cent of the business with her husband, who now works full-time for the company. She thinks the secret of her success is attention to detail.

She says: 'If something isn't quite right for a client I am like a dog with a bone. I need to know why and to find out what we can do to make it right. I get a real buzz if clients are delighted with what we provide.'

She has this advice for budding entrepreneurs: 'Follow your dreams. If you really feel that you want to do something then just do it. But put all your effort into making it successful. If you work hard now then you can play in years to come.'

17

Start networking

The concept of networking can strike fear into the hearts of even the boldest budding entrepreneur. It is perhaps not surprising. Networking is basically all about putting yourself out there and telling complete strangers who you are and what you do – and what you need – in quite an upfront way. And that can be pretty scary, particularly when you are just starting out in business and are not really sure yourself of the answers to any of the above.

The secret is to stop thinking of it as networking and start thinking about it in a less confrontational way. Heather Gorringe, the founder of Wiggly Wigglers, which makes and sells worm composters, says: 'I never think of myself as networking. To me it is about listening and having a conversation. It is about what you can do to help others because people you help are far more likely to try to do things in return for you.'

Whatever you want to call it, networking is worth persevering with because it can be a fantastic way of meeting other like-minded people in your situation, in your industry, or in your local region. It can bring you together with people you would never have met otherwise who may end up being your suppliers, your distributors and your customers.

Traditional networking events include breakfast meetings, lunches and speaker evenings and you will find a variety of them being run each month by business groups such as the British Chambers of Commerce, Business Link and your local enterprise agency. A big conference event will often be sponsored by several business agencies together. They are a great place to start networking and it can be a great relief to discover people like you who are also in the early stages of starting up a business.

Once you have attended a networking event and got a feel for how it works, try to get it to work in the best way possible for you. For example, you could ring the organisers and offer to speak about your own experiences trying to start up a business. That way not only will you be able to attend the event for free, you will significantly raise your profile and stand out from the crowd so that afterwards people will approach you, rather than the other way round.

Duncan Cheatle, who runs The Supper Club for entrepreneurs in London, says networking has other benefits too: 'It can be quite lonely running a business. Many of the issues you can't discuss with your spouse or friends, or even your board of directors if you have one. Networking is a great way of trying out your business pitch and of building your confidence.'

If the idea of attending a breakfast meeting at 7.30 am somewhere off the M6 is really not for you, the good news is that there are now lots of different ways to network. Every month, for example, Oli Barrett, an internet entrepreneur, hosts a free speed-networking event somewhere in Britain. Forty people are given just three minutes to chat to someone before a whistle is blown and they must talk to someone else.

Barrett says: 'One of the things I found frustrating about the business networking events I went to was that they were too industry-specific. When you are starting a new business you need all sorts of people to make it work – you need lawyers, accountants, investors, customers and PR people. The other thing that annoyed me about the events was that they were far too stagnant. I thought they needed mixing up a bit.'

He deliberately invites a wide range of people to his events, in the belief that diversity is more likely to spark off interesting conversation. 'In my experience the best ideas come when people from very different backgrounds mix together', he says. 'People who come wanting to do a specific deal go away disappointed, but people who come seeking new ideas and fresh perspectives from interesting people really enjoy it.'

You can even network online. It does lack the personal contact that can be so important in making a connection, but the advantage is that you can meet people from all over the country rather than just in your local area.

Peter Bennett, the founder of the Ozone Business Network, a virtual networking service, says: 'The traditional organisations such as Chambers of Commerce tend to offer fairly unstructured ways to network. Breakfast networks are more structured and more focused on finding mutual referrals, but these still involve people who live within a few miles of each other. They work very well for businesses that are geographically limited in their scope, such as a builder's merchant. Virtual networks are ideal for people in the professional services industries or for entrepreneurs looking to find like-minded people and build businesses quickly.'

Heather Gorringe of Wiggly Wigglers says she finds online networking a much more enjoyable way of forming connections with other business people than face to face. She says: 'I think of networking as a bunch of men in suits each given a minute to talk about their business and then eating unpleasant fried food. I'm terrible at striking up conversations with people in these situations as I'm always afraid I'll be wasting their time.'

The bottom line is that networking is not just about handing out a load of business cards and hoping that in a few weeks' time someone will discover your card in a jacket pocket and somehow remember who you are and what you do. Or gathering a list of e-mails and sending out updates about your business. It is about making a real connection with someone – and discovering how you can mutually benefit and help each other. And that can happen anywhere and anytime. At a party, on the beach, even standing at the bus stop. Tommy Schweiger, the founder of Character World, which makes bedding for Argos and other stores featuring children's television characters such as Thomas the Tank Engine, landed his first big contract after bumping into the merchandising director of Manchester United football club at a swimming pool. The two men, who had never met before, got talking about what they did and as a result Schweiger landed a six-year contract to supply all Manchester United's non-football related merchandising.

You just have to get into habit of talking to people about yourself at every opportunity. And listening to what they have to say in return.

Top tip

If you are attending a conference find out in advance who is going to be there and contact the people you would like to meet beforehand to arrange a time to chat. Do not rely on bumping into them.

Profile: Neil Duttson, founder of Duttson Rocks

Six months in the Royal Marines followed by six years working as a DJ at parties is perhaps not the most obvious route to starting up a business selling diamonds. Fortunately Neil Duttson has always been extremely good at networking.

He says: 'I think my personality, and the fact that I know what I am talking about, accounts for a large percentage of my sales. I can walk into a room and as long as my personality wins a guy over – it is normally men I deal with because they are the ones buying engagement rings – I will probably have that sale.'

Duttson spent his early childhood years overseas as his father was in the Royal Marines, then moved with his family to Ramsgate, Kent, when he was seven. He did not concentrate at school and left at 16, having taken nine O levels and failed them all.

He joined the Royal Marines as his father had before him but quickly realised it was not for him. So he left and spent the next two and a half years working his way around the world. He ended up in the French skiing resort of Val D'Isere where he got a job as a DJ in a nightclub and stayed two seasons.

Then he came back to London and got a job with Juliana's, an events management company that provided DJs and marquees for parties. After six years though, and by now 26, Duttson realised it was not something he wanted to do as a career for the rest of his life.

It was at this point he began to think about starting up his own diamond business. He says: 'I had always had a passion for diamonds. When I was 18 I bought a book on gemology but I had never actually done anything about it.' He also thought working in the diamond industry might provide lots of travel opportunities.

He explored the idea of working for De Beers, one of the biggest diamond companies in the world, but they required two A levels to join their training course. So Duttson, who had no qualifications, realised he needed to find another route into the industry.

He searched on the internet and found a school in Antwerp, Belgium, run by the HRD (Diamond High Council) that ran a six-month course in diamonds. Having no savings he remortgaged his flat, which he had bought while working as a DJ, and took out £50,000 of the equity to pay for the course and support himself while doing it.

It was a bold step to take but he loved it. He says: 'I realised that I could do the maths, physics and chemistry which I couldn't do at school. At the weekends I travelled around Europe, going into jewellery shops pretending I was getting engaged to find out what they charged. It was a total change. In fact it was a complete re-invention of my life and that was what really excited me.'

He took more courses in synthetic diamonds and man-made stones to make sure he knew what he was talking about. He says: 'A lot of friends were getting engaged and said they would give me a chance to find them a ring – but pointed out that six months ago I was putting up marquees. So I had to prove myself.'

Armed with his knowledge of diamonds, Duttson set about setting himself up in business as a diamond jeweller. It proved to be a lot harder than he thought. He says: 'The diamond industry is quite a dark and mysterious industry and knowing where to buy diamonds was a real hurdle. It actually took ages to gain the trust of dealers. I went to a jewellery fair in Basle in Switzerland and basic-ally went round every stand telling dealers what I was doing and that I wanted to buy from them. I got a lot of closed doors.'

After four months, however, he eventually met two dealers, one in Israel and one in Antwerp, who were prepared to do business with him. They are still his suppliers today.

After finding rings for friends who were getting engaged, word of mouth gradually brought more customers, helped by Duttson's talent for networking. He says: 'I am very good at talking to people. When someone asks me at a dinner party what I do for a living it is a big talking point. People love to know where diamonds come from. I can convert about 90 per cent of the people I talk to into a sale.'

Without the funds to buy any stock, Duttson would show potential customers a selection of glass fakes in every single cut and shape of diamond. Only once they had chosen and paid a deposit would he actually purchase the real diamond. Then he got a jeweller friend in Kent to set the diamonds into rings. Because he did not have actual diamond rings for people to choose from, Duttson developed the concept of someone proposing with just a diamond in a box so that the lady could decide what sort of ring she wanted at a later date.

There were some setbacks on the way, however. He says: 'The worst mistake I ever made was I employed someone who stayed with me for six months and learnt everything he needed to know – and then disappeared and set up his own business in competition taking two of my designers.' The man is no longer in business.

Duttson Rocks is a member of the Kimberley Process, which means that he only buys diamonds from legitimate sources and not those involved in funding conflicts. As well as rings Duttson now also sells bracelets, necklaces and earrings and in 2007 brought out his first collection of designs. He now has his own workshop in London's Hatton Garden and turnover in 2008 is expected to be £5 million.

Now 40, Duttson says the secret to being a successful networker is very simple: 'It is about making people comfortable in your presence. Because otherwise people can get quite bored quite quickly.'

18

Build a strong team around you

When you start your own business you are probably going to be doing everything yourself. Not just the obvious stuff such as answering phones, dealing with suppliers and packing the products but all the other tasks too such as crawling round to find the gas meter, finding out how the photocopier works and trying to fix a leaking roof. Some of these tasks will come naturally to you, others much less so.

At some point, however, all successful entrepreneurs need to do something they find even more difficult than any of these – they need to learn how to let go and pass some responsibility on to other people. While the popular image of the entrepreneur might be of the solitary figure striding forth, in reality the successful ones have built a strong team of people around them to help and support them.

There are three reasons for this. The first is that there are only 24 hours in the day and no matter how dedicated you are to your business, you cannot be in two places at once.

The second reason is that if the business is to grow you need to create space for yourself to think about the bigger picture of where your company is heading and what it needs to do to get there. And you cannot do that if you are spending every waking hour trying to find the manual to work out how the photocopier functions. The third reason is that of the 101 tasks you are currently doing in your business you are probably only going to be any good at 30 per cent of them so it makes a lot more sense to get other more skilled people to do the bits you are hopeless at.

Mark Riminton, Director of Shirlaws, a business-coaching company, says: 'Entrepreneurs have a fear of letting go of things. They worry about whether something will be done properly and whether the business will fall over. But businesses simply can't grow beyond a certain point with the average entrepreneur still in place.'

It may sound strange but your aim from the very first moment of starting up your business should be to make yourself redundant. While it might be flattering to be indispensable, it is not the way to run a successful business.

The first step is to write a manual for every single task you perform in the company, from answering the phone to filling in an invoice, no matter how trivial it seems. Then delegate that task to someone else. That someone else may be an employee or it may be an outside agency to whom you can outsource a particular function, for example doing your accounts or packing and dispatching the products. What you are aiming to do is get to a stage where you can be confident that the business will continue to function well even when you are not there.

Riminton says the solution is to create structures within the firm so that responsibility can be spread. 'Put in place systems that encourage employees to take responsibility for tasks in the business rather than them being told to do something', he says. 'Try to create an environment where people feel able to step forward and say: "I would like to do that".'

If you do not, you can end up seriously limiting your company's growth. One of Riminton's clients was so reluctant to let go that he had an in-tray full of things people wanted him to do, but he could not do them because he was so overloaded with other tasks.

'There was a lot of frustration in the business that things weren't getting done because he couldn't get round to doing them', says Riminton. 'His personal life was completely overwhelmed by his business because he was working seven days a week and still feeling he couldn't keep up with everything, so he was experiencing a great deal of stress and frustration in his life.' After the client delegated much of his workload, the company's turnover doubled and he was able to free up enough spare time to pursue interests outside the business.

Daniel Ronen, director of DoS UK, a business consultancy, says the ultimate aim should be to work yourself out of a job. 'Your aim should be to structure the company so that everything is being done without your personal day-to-day involvement.'

The way to do this, he says, is to look at the things you do each day and work out which of them can be delegated. 'If you don't let go you will never grow', he says. 'It is like asking whether Sir Richard Branson pilots his 747s or fixes the engines. No he doesn't, he delegates those tasks to other people.'

Jane Shepherd, the founder of Organics for Kids, which makes clothes for children up to the age of two, realised early on that she could not hope to do everything herself in her business. So she decided to concentrate on the things she did best and get other people to do the rest. She now designs the clothes herself and buys 'fair trade' organic cotton from overseas, but has outsourced the manufacturing to a company in Nottingham and has other goods made in India. She is also in the process of outsourcing her sales operation. 'Selling is not my strength. I am just about to start working with an agent who will visit shops round the country, which I can't do on my own. By working with an agent I don't need to employ sales staff', she says.

Kim Fletcher, an adviser with Business Link in Kent, says the secret to creating a strong team is to take things one step at a time. 'Don't take on 10 people at once. Take on one part-timer and work out what you are good at and what you are not good at.'

'A lot of people think that delegation is about sitting at a desk and ordering people about in some sort of Dickensian way. But it isn't – it is about ensuring that people know what you are trying to do and what the business is trying to do and ensuring that they are all aligned with what you want them to do.'

Top tip

Write down everything you do in half-hour segments over two weeks. Then decide which are the tasks only you can do – and which are the ones you could get someone else to do.

Profile: Sean Phelan, founder of Multimap

Sean Phelan was introduced to the idea of becoming an entrepreneur from a young age. Both his parents had started up businesses – his father had a company that supplied high-end restaurants and his mother ran a ballet school. 'When I was a child all the dinner conversation was about small businesses and being nice to customers', he says.

Born and brought up in North London with his brother and sister, Phelan's first attempts at making money came at the age of 11 when he sold stink bombs at school. He would also develop friends' photos in his darkroom in the basement at home.

After taking A levels, Phelan was sponsored by Marconi to study engineering and computer science at Sussex University. He worked for the company for a year and then during the summer holidays. He then joined a software consultancy. He spent 18 months there and then went to work for a Canadian company, where he stayed for seven years.

At the age of 30, however, Phelan had a moment of awakening when the company ran out of money and was rescued by venture capitalists. 'This smart, personable Canadian guy was brought in to run the company and he was 31 years old, only a year older than me', says Phelan. 'He was doing exactly what I wanted to be doing and I realised I couldn't get to where he was from where I was. He had an MBA from Insead, the French business school. It really focused me.'

Phelan quit his job and took a full-time MBA course in the south of France for a year. He loved it. Then he got a job with a telecoms consultancy called the Yankee Group. While he was there he started to seriously consider the idea of starting up his own business. At the age of 37, he quit his full-time job and took a part-time consulting contract with the Yankee Group for a year instead. This enabled him to work on his own venture for half the week and also provided him with £60,000 seed money to start his own business.

Phelan's initial plan was to use the technology of GSM phones and GPS satellite systems to put maps on mobile phones. But when the internet suddenly took off he realised that the future lay there. 'I remember thinking at the time that I had missed the PC revolution and I did not want to miss the internet revolution. Now was the time to do it. It was put up or shut up. One of the many important lessons I learnt on my MBA programme was that successful entrepreneurs follow the money.'

His Multimap website went live in 1997 and Phelan quickly realised that there were two ways of making money from it – by advertising on his own website and by providing maps for other businesses to use on their sites. As the internet became more popular, businesses such as estate agents realised that they needed maps on their websites to show customers where the houses for sale were located. Retail businesses needed to show people where to find their stores.

Initially, Phelan ran the business from home and outsourced as much of the work as he could. 'On the MBA programme I learnt that for a cash-strapped start-up, variable costs are OK and fixed costs are bad. So I outsourced the hosting of the servers to an internet service provider, I outsourced the advertising sales and I outsourced the book-keeping to my accountant.'

Three years after the business was launched it was doing so well that when Phelan, who was still running it single-handedly, approached investors he managed to sell a 25 per cent stake in the company for almost £1.9 million. The first thing Phelan and his new investor did was to start recruiting staff. 'Up to that point I had no staff at all', he says. 'I was answering the phone, taking sales calls and doing support during the day. I was writing code in the evenings. I was installing software at weekends. It was exhausting.'

He started to build a team around him and as a result Multimap has developed a reputation for being a company where employees are encouraged to develop ideas of their own. When one of the company's Australian employees, Ian Dodds, was asked by a customer to solve a particular problem, for example, he went one better and created a new way of displaying complex shapes on maps. The idea was taken up by the company and has now been rolled out across Multimap's entire global operations. Multimap's turnover in 2008 is expected to be substantially more than 2007's turnover figure of £12 million.

Now aged 50, Phelan thinks the secret of his success is recruiting good people and knowing when to delegate. He says: 'A lot of entrepreneurial start-ups grow very rapidly and then stagnate because the founder doesn't want to let anything out of the door without having personally checked it. That limits growth because it means they don't develop middle management, and the people they do have working for them aren't motivated because they feel they are being checked up on all the time. One has to create an environment that is attractive and exciting to work in and where people feel they can realise their goals.'

Phelan, who now owns 50 per cent of the business after accounting for employee share-options, has this advice for budding entrepreneurs: 'Start on the cheap and in the early days spend as little money as possible. But also be on the lookout from day one for really good people to work with. Find them, motivate them and retain them and give them the wherewithal to do their job. Good people will want to join a start-up if they believe in it.'

However, he also warns: 'In the early days don't recruit people who are just like yourself. You want people whose strengths complement your weaknesses.'

19

Learn from your mistakes

The first time Trinny Woodall and Susannah Constantine, now highly successful fashion experts best known for their television show *What Not to Wear*, tried going into business together they started up a clothing website called Ready2Shop at the height of the dotcom boom. Unfortunately when that boom turned to bust their business went from being valued at £10 million to being virtually worthless in the space of a few weeks. They and their backers lost everything.

Failure is a horrible word. It reeks of sadness and despair and of staring down into a very black hole. For many would-be entrepreneurs the fear of failure is one of the biggest factors holding them back from taking the plunge and starting up their own business. It is hardly surprising – failure can mean not only losing everything you have, your home and savings, your confidence and self-belief. It can also mean humiliation, both publicly and amongst those friends and family who always thought you were mad to try anyway.

Unfortunately for entrepreneurs failure is virtually an occupational hazard. With statistics showing that two thirds of all start-ups fail in the first three years, it is more than likely that you will come up against failure at some point. And those who have several successful ventures behind them are no more immune than first-time entrepreneurs. But while repeated and persistent failure is of no use to anyone, discovering how *not* to do something can actually be far more useful in the long run than doing it the right way first time.

Indeed Mark Loftus of OCG, a business psychology consultancy, thinks that early failure might be closely linked to ultimate success. He says: 'For people to succeed in business it is almost essential to fail first. They gain a depth of resilience that comes from failing and then recovering from that failure. In fact, if an entrepreneur who hadn't had many setbacks hit a big setback, it might completely derail them.'

So how do you go about learning from your mistakes without letting them engulf your soul? The first step in dealing with failure is not to take it personally. Remember, it was the business that failed, not you.

Kim Fletcher, an adviser with Business Link in Kent, says: 'You need to be able to detach yourself from it. If you regard failure as being something personal, you will not be able to take a step outside it and look at it dispassionately. You have to be able to say, did I make the right decision or the wrong decision? What information didn't I have that would have helped me make a better decision that would not have taken me down this route?'

He says a vital element of being able to learn from your mistakes is analysing the type of failure you experienced so you can find out the reason for it. Normally, on closer inspection, it will be obvious what caused it. 'Is it a failure because you lost money, or because you lost a customer, or because you lost a person in your business? Perhaps you were far too engaged in the technology at the expense of delivering what the customer wanted?

'Perhaps you didn't have sufficient finance to make the product or be able to survive long enough to get the product to market. Or you got the quality wrong or the timing was wrong or you didn't have the right skills to get it to market. Or the product was behind the curve or it was the wrong price or you weren't approaching people in the right way.'

If you find it impossible to dispassionately analyse the reasons for failure, you should enlist outside help. Sometimes talking it through with someone from outside the business can really help you pinpoint where it all went wrong.

Daniel Ronen, director of DoS UK, a business consultancy, says the big benefit of making a mistake is that it gives you time to reflect: 'Failure forces you to stop, look, think and act. That is the cycle everyone should be doing in business. The problem is that people are so busy doing what they are doing that they do not stop and take a hard look at what is working, what is not working and what needs to change. But with failure you are actually forced to stop what you are doing and start thinking about it again.'

The secret is to ignore your detractors and concentrate on seeing your failures as your own personal lessons in business success. And try not to be so hard on yourself. 'Very few people are born brilliant business people', says Ronen. 'Failing forces you to stop what you were doing and look at what went wrong. You need to be resilient. Try to focus on the bigger picture and on what you want to achieve. If you can, leverage some of the good things you have done and bring them with you.'

In other words, how much you are able to learn from your failure and take something useful away from the situation has a lot to do with your attitude towards it, and towards yourself for having got into the situation in the first place. Simply blaming yourself – or blaming other people – for what happened has no lasting benefit and is likely to prevent you from letting go and moving on.

Finally, if your business does start to fail, one of the best ways to ensure you bounce back relatively unscathed is to make the most of support mechanisms around you, such as family and friends. If you feel that your whole life is crumbling around you, rather than just your business, it can be much harder to believe that it is possible to bounce back. Being surrounded by people who love you regardless can play a big part in helping you keep a sense of perspective – and even a much needed sense of humour.

As Mark Riminton, Director of Shirlaws, a business-coaching company, puts it: 'Entrepreneurs often feel that they have to deal with failure on their own. But – and this is often the hardest part for many people – they need to put their hand up and say they could really do with some help. Ultimately, failure is really just a feeling. So if you are able to tune into that feeling early, then what feels like failure may simply be another step on the way to success.'

Top tip

Remember that it was the business that
failed, not you.

Profile: David Speakman, founder of Travel Counsellors

David Speakman's entrepreneurial instinct kicked in early. By the age of 12 he was buying comics and renting them out to friends at school to make extra pocket money. Adopted as a baby, he was brought up in a small terraced house in south Lancashire, where his adoptive father was a miner in one of the local pits. He left school at 16 with a few O levels, went to building college and then became a quantity surveyor with a building firm.

He says: 'I remember the careers master at school telling me there were eight types of surveying. I asked him which one paid the most and when he said quantity surveying I said: "Right I'll do that".'

After a few years, when he had worked his way up the firm, he asked his boss if he could have a stake in the company. The owner refused and so, at the age of 30, Speakman handed in his notice and left to start his own business. He did not have the contacts to open his own quantity-surveying firm, so he and his wife sold their house and bought an off-licence in the nearby town of Atherton. They lived above the shop with their two children and gradually took the business upmarket by adding a delicatessen.

One day a customer mentioned that he wanted to open a travel agency in the town. Speakman decided it was a great idea and offered to finance him. The two opened the agency in a former tobacconist. But his partner lasted just three months, so Speakman, who by now had sold the off-licence, took over the travel agency and ran it himself.

Over the next few years he built up the business until it had five shops and a turnover of £8 million a year. However, by 1986, when Speakman was 40, he decided it was time for a change and sold the firm. He says: 'As an entrepreneur I get bored and I want to move on. I don't want to jump through the same hoops every year.'

Speakman decided his next move would be to open a large travel company in a warehouse, funding it with £500,000 of his own money and venture capital of £1 million. He asked Greenalls Breweries to show him some properties. But when he was shown a pub that could be converted he was so taken with it that he decided to open a themed restaurant instead. 'It just inspired me', he says. 'I thought I could make a fantastic American restaurant there.'

He went home and told his wife Maureen what he planned to do. He says: 'She said she trusted me and believed I could do anything I wanted to do. I sincerely believe that if you are supported like that then you can take on the world.' He spent a total of £430,000 setting up the restaurant and it was so successful that 10 months later he sold it for £930,000, making himself a £500,000 profit. 'We had the right thing at the right time', he says.

He opened another travel agency in Atherton and, enthused by his previous success, decided in 1989 to open another restaurant. But this time he picked the wrong location. He says: 'It was a terrible site. Then the Gulf war started, there was a fire on the roof within the first two months, the motorway junction that led to the restaurant was closed, and the guy who was in partnership with me quit after three months.'

Speakman took over his former partner's shares and tried to make the best of the situation, but it was no good. In 1994 he was forced to give the property back to the bank. He lost all the money he had made in his career, including the profits from selling his travel agency and his first restaurant.

He says: 'I lost at least £1 million. The worst thing was I felt I had let my family down. We had been quite well off, but now we had the humbling experience of having to borrow money from people. Two of my children were at private school but I couldn't afford to send the third one. It was a terrible feeling.'

His one hope was the little travel agency. Determined not to repeat his earlier mistakes, Speakman decided the best way forward was to start small. Because he had no capital, he chose to create a new kind of travel firm, getting people to work from home on a commission-only basis. 'We equipped people with laptop computers so that they could visit customers at home and sell travel,' he says. 'They built up their own customer base from friends and family and referrals.'

Sales immediately took off, but profit was harder to come by. Just before Christmas 1996, two years after he had started the company, the bank was ready to pull the plug. But Speakman persuaded it to wait. By the following summer Travel Counsellors was back on track. It is now the largest home-based company in the world, with 850 self-employed counsellors across seven countries who between them generate £210 million of business.

Speakman, who owns 100 per cent of the Bolton-based firm, thinks the secret of his success is focus. He says: 'As an entrepreneur if you are not careful you can have 50 ideas a day. But I realised very quickly that Travel Counsellors was something special.'

He has also been careful to learn from his mistakes. 'I just want to be the best', he says. 'One of the things I really regretted with the failure of the restaurant was that I lost five years of my business life. I love business because it is like chess. I love winning.'

20

Accept that it will always take longer than you think

When British student Alex Pew launched his Million dollar home page (www.milliondollarhomepage.com) on the internet with the aim of selling the space on a single web page to advertisers by the pixel, it took him just four months to make a profit of more than US $1 million. Unfortunately Pew is the exception that proves the rule. The reality is that most entrepreneurs take a great deal longer to make their fortune – not just weeks or months but years and years.

The idea of overnight success is highly alluring. The media particularly loves the concept and scarcely a day goes by without a business being described as being an overnight success. One minute the budding entrepreneur is sitting at their desk staring at a blank piece of paper, the next they are heading up a fast-growing business and heading for the stratosphere.

Sadly the truth is rather more prosaic. While the occasional entrepreneur does manage to seize an opportunity and run with it in the space of weeks, most fledgling entrepreneurs can realistically expect a stretch of at least three years from having the idea to having a business that is properly up and running – and often much, much longer.

Katie Moore, Managing Partner of Business Startup Community (www.startupcommunity.co.uk), an online information exchange for entrepreneurs, says: 'Generally speaking to get a business started up will take a good three years. And if you look at the history of a lot of successful entrepreneurs, success comes 10, 20 years down the line. It is very rare that somebody does so well in their business that they will break even after a year. It doesn't happen overnight.'

Professor Martin Binks, Director of the University of Nottingham Institute for Enterprise and Innovation at Nottingham University Business School, says the time it takes to start up a business can differ markedly depending on what type of business you are setting up and in what type of industry. Retail, for example, will be a lot quicker than biotech. But he too agrees that the concept of overnight success is largely a myth.

'Often what looks like overnight success is actually the culmination of a lot of market research and preparation, checking out locations, skills and availability and finance. Or it is long-accumulated tactical knowledge that is deployed independently through having worked for somebody else.'

There are two main phases to starting up a business – the time spent preparing and researching before the launch, and the time spent getting the venture up and running following the launch. Both parts always take at least twice as long as you think they will – not because you are procrastinating or being hopeless, but because often you are reliant on other people playing their part in a timetable they did not write.

Dr Glenn Crocker is the co-founder and Director of R5 Pharmaceuticals, based in Nottingham, which manufactures pharmaceuticals under contract. It took him 18 months from having the idea for the business to launching it at the end of 2006, and he expects it to take another 18 months until the business breaks even. In his case the planning phase stretched out beyond his initial expectations because of a number of factors. Simply writing the business plan for his venture took four to five months, and then it took another seven months just to get the bank to agree to provide a loan.

He says: 'The banks can be incredibly slow. They keep coming back asking you for more information which you feel is completely irrelevant, and sometimes you get right to the very end of the application process and then somebody 300 miles away in head office will decide they don't want to do this after all. So you have to go to the next bank and start all over again.'

His strategy for survival is to measure progress in small units. 'You need to think of successes as very small steps otherwise you would give up well before the end. Things like recruiting a great person and getting the first contract.'

So how do you go about preparing for the several years of hard slog and grind it is going to take to get your business onto an even keel? The first step is to have a sound business plan and to keep referring back to it. Moore says: 'If you are looking to start a business the ultimate tool you can have is business planning. Without having a business plan which looks over a five year sustainability programme I don't think people should even think about starting a business. About 80 per cent of businesses fail within five years and I think a vast amount of that is due to lack of planning and lack of foresight.'

And it is not enough just to write a business plan – you need to keep referring back to it again and again. Things can change constantly when you are starting up a business so it is very important that you keep looking back at your business plan and use it as a reference guide. When you are in the throes of starting up a business and trying to do a million different things at once, it can be astonishingly easy to forget the work and fact-finding you did at the beginning when you were starting out. It is only by checking your business plan that you can keep on track with what is going on and how the business is developing.

The second step is to talk to people who have done it before you. Moore says: 'Mix with people who are in a similar position to you, people who are inspired and motivated to be entrepreneurs. There is no substitute for talking to other people and learning from their mistakes.'

The third step is to learn the art of being patient. When you are starting up a business it can be immensely frustrating to discover that the world around you – bank managers, suppliers, local council officials, landlords, health and safety inspectors – are not immediately going to drop everything they were doing and sort things out for you. But the fact is they are not going to. Standard processes, particularly those involving councils, red tape and bureaucracy, are generally going to take as long as they always take and if you can approach the whole exercise in a spirit of cheerful resignation then you are going to save yourself a lot of agonised wailing and futile fury.

Top tip

Be realistic. It takes at least three years to get from idea to break-even point so think about how you are going to support yourself financially and emotionally during this time.

Profile: Edward Perry, founder of Cook

Edward Perry has been nothing if not persistent in his determination to make his business work. His frozen ready meals business, Cook, took ten years to make its first profit – and for the first two years in business as a sole trader Perry did not even bother keeping accounts because they were so bad. He says: 'I am sure if I had kept accounts lots of worthy people would have said I needed to shut the business down. So I ignored the truth and kept going.'

Born and brought up in Maidenhead, Berkshire in a family of four children, Perry saw at first hand both the attractions and perils of starting up a small business. When he was 10 his father left his secure job as headmaster of a prep school and his parents opened two small coffee shops. They just about managed to support the family from the venture but it was hard work.

Perry started helping out in the coffee shops from the age of 14 and when he left school at the age of 18 he briefly sold advertising space for a national newspaper. But he hated it and after nine months went to work for his parents, running a small shop attached to a bakery they had set up. While he was there he started thinking about the idea of starting up a business of his own selling high-quality frozen ready meals. He says: 'I thought that the quality the supermarkets were producing was awful and that there had to be a better way.'

He was not interested in making ready meals to sell to other shops, however. He wanted to sell them only through retail shops of his own. In 1996, by now 25, he asked his parents whether they would be interested in doing ready meals as part of the family business. They said no.

Undaunted, Perry persuaded one of the bakery's customers, a chef called Dale Penfold, to help him pursue his vision. With no savings of his own Perry took out a £15,000 bank loan, Penfold got a £5,000 loan and Perry borrowed £5,000 from his parents, providing a total of £25,000 to get the business off the ground.

Perry rented a kitchen in Kent where Penfold could prepare the food and found a shop in Farnham to rent for £10,000 a year. Then, full of confidence, he asked Penfold to prepare a large batch of three recipes using the same ingredients and techniques that people would use to prepare the dishes in their kitchens at home.

It was at this point that the idea started to unravel. Perry says: 'I really genuinely believed that the meals Dale produced would be fantastic from day one. But I heated up the dishes in my flat and they were inedible – and we had just made 200 portions of each of them. I sat on the stairs and cried.'

In the end it took three months to devise a handful of dishes they could actually sell, such as beef bourguignon and fish pie. The delay meant that initially their shop had very little to offer customers.

The two of them gradually got a complete range of ready meals together that they could sell in the shop and a friend opened a second Cook shop in Tunbridge Wells. But Perry admits that the first three years were miserable. He says: 'They were a battle of grim survival. It was awful. We weren't selling much and it was totally hand to mouth.'

By the end of 1999 the business had a turnover of £500,000 but Perry realised he needed further investment in order to move into a larger kitchen. The bank refused to lend him any more money. But he was convinced the business had potential so he talked over the problem with his younger brother James who was by now running his parents' coffee shop and bakery business, which had a turnover of £1.5 million. James suggested that Perry and his parents merge their businesses together. Perry says: 'I said you have got to be joking, you must be mad. We talked about this back in 1997, you all said no and here you are trying to do a merger again.'

It was not long, however, before he realised it could be a good idea. So in 2000 they put the two businesses together. After three years they sold both coffee shops and the bakery business in order to invest the £1 million the sales raised in Cook, as everyone in the family believed it had the greater potential. He says: 'My parents made an enormous leap of faith because Cook was just this tiny business which was losing money, and they had built up a nice business which was doing quite well and was their pension.'

However, with investment in larger kitchens and more shops Cook took off. In 2006 Perry and the family also sold 12 per cent of the business for just over £1 million to two private investors, enabling yet more investment in the business. Cook now has 21 shops and in 2008 is expected to have a turnover of £18 million. The business has also started selling its frozen ready meals via concessions in farm shops.

The one thing Perry is still not completely happy about is the name. He initially called the shop Cakes and Casseroles but in 2000 changed it to Cook. 'It was at the time when one-word snappy titles were in vogue. But Cook is not a good name. It is a bit corporate and doesn't fit with our ethos. We should have put our names above the door.'

Now 37 and married with a child, Perry thinks the secret of his success is perseverance and self-belief: 'I always believed it would work, no matter how much everything indicated that it was not working.'

His advice to budding entrepreneurs is this: 'It is vital that you enjoy yourself. People say you should never fall in love with your business – but there are quite a few of us who are completely in love with this business. I think life is far too short to be doing something you don't enjoy.'

Appendix:
Useful websites

British Business Angels Association
www.bbaa.org.uk

British Chambers of Commerce
www.chamberonline.co.uk

British Library Business and Intellectual Property Centre
www.bl.uk/bipc

British Private Equity and Venture Capital Association
www.bvca.co.uk

Business Link
Government-backed advice centre for businesses
www.businesslink.gov.uk

Chartered Institute of Patent Agents
www.cipa.org.uk

Companies House
www.companieshouse.gov.uk

Department for Business Enterprise and Regulatory Reform
www.berr.gov.uk

GrantsNet
Searchable database of UK grants, loans and funding schemes
www.grantsnet.co.uk

Health and Safety Executive
www.hse.gov.uk

HM Revenue and Customs
www.hmrc.gov.uk

Horsesmouth
Online business mentoring network
www.horsesmouth_.co.uk

Learn Direct
Online learning network
www.learndirect.co.uk

National Federation of Enterprise Agencies
www.nfea.com

Princes Trust Business Programme
Advice and loans for 18–30-year-olds starting up a business
www.princes-trust.org.uk

Shell Livewire
Free start-up business advice for 16–30-year-olds
www.shell-livewire.org

UK Intellectual Property Office
www.ipo.gov.uk

ALSO AVAILABLE FROM KOGAN PAGE

ISBN: 978 0 7494 4311 5   Hardback   2004

"I am delighted that a new generation of entrepreneurs is emerging whose ideas and innovation will provide the momentum to drive business in this country forward. Rachel Bridge's inspiring book has perfectly summed up the passion, the commitment and the sheer excitement of being an entrepreneur and will help encourage many others to do the same."

Sir Richard Branson

"A book for the bedside table to be read at bedtime so one can dream... an excellent gift for the aspiring businessman or woman... an easy and pleasurable read."

Personnel Today

"Lively, inspiring portraits show that there is no recipe for success: they have all achieved their goals through a very personal route."

Business Plus

"Should make inspiring reading for any wage slave who is stuck in a rut."

Accounting & Business

"A collection of 40 of the best stories of ideas and innovation from the world of growing business."

MBA Business

"Read this book to inspire you when the going gets tough, to reassure you when you've run out of ideas and to give you a kick up the backside when you are feeling sorry for yourself. But whatever you do – read it."

Reading Chronicle

"Inspiring stories of people who have made their fortunes through innovation and entrepreneurship, sometimes against all odds."

Edge

Order online now at www.koganpage.com

Sign up for regular e-mail updates on new
Kogan Page books in your interest area

ALSO AVAILABLE FROM KOGAN PAGE

ISBN: 978 0 7494 4626 0   Hardback   2006

Order online now at www.koganpage.com

Sign up for regular e-mail updates on new
Kogan Page books in your interest area

"Every entrepreneur needs a big idea and Rachel Bridge's inspiring second book brilliantly captures the challenge, frustration and excitement of turning a big idea into a successful business. Essential reading for every budding entrepreneur."
Sir Richard Branson

"Throws light on the sort of person it takes to succeed as an entrepreneur."
Management Today

"Serves as a quiet reminder that with enough determination, a little imagination and a spot of good luck, anything is possible."
Quality World

"An insight into innovative thought processes."
One Step

"Explains where to find the most promising business ideas and crucially, how to determine if they will sell."
Personal Success

"Rather than dredging up the usual throng of software and banking kingpins, the individuals interviewed have taken rather more unusual routes to financial reward... The book advises, right from the start, that having a good idea can often be as simple and finding a solution to something you find annoying, then branding or reworking it."
EasyJet